# Executive Summary

Those responsible for education and professional development within systems such as corporations, state governments, and government agencies are concerned about the quality of those opportunities. As a result, they increasingly assign responsibility for ensuring the quality and productivity of education within the system to one particular office or agency. Often, such agencies receive little guidance about how to approach their task.

A RAND research team conducted a broad review of the general literature on the assessment of quality and productivity in education and professional development. The team also reviewed the documentation of organizations engaged in such assessment, interviewed experts, attended conferences, and conducted site visits to exemplary organizations. This report synthesizes that information and provides suggestions for approaches that might be useful for agencies given the task of ensuring the quality and productivity of education and professional development activities in a specific system. (*Assessment* as used in this monograph means the start-to-finish process of examining quality or productivity, while *evaluation* is the step in the assessment process in which performance measures are examined and a judgment about performance is made on the basis of that examination.)

## Why Is System-Level Assessment Needed?

Although the main task of assessment focuses on the quality and productivity of specific providers of education and professional development, the study found that a higher-level assessment of the system as a whole is also crucial.

Such an assessment has two main purposes: (1) to determine whether the stakeholder and system-level needs are being addressed, and (2) to identify opportunities to improve efficiency in existing programs. In the first case, system-level assessment compares the needs of the population served with the programs offered in the system. In a corporate setting, for example, such an assessment might find that certain corporate-level goals are not being addressed by education and training programs run by individual business units. In higher education, a system-level assessment might find that certain geographical regions are not being well served by existing institutions in a state.

To achieve the second aim, the assessment examines whether the system's resources are being allocated efficiently. A number of organizations are improving their productivity through this process.

- The Texas Higher Education Coordinating Board conducts regular program reviews to assess whether a proposed program is based on established needs, whether it duplicates other programs in the same area, and whether it falls within an institution's mission.
- At Lucent Technologies, corporate oversight has streamlined education and professional development by assessing whether limited education and training resources are being used in a way that promotes overall corporate goals. The focus on business needs rather than student demand allowed them to reduce the number of courses taught throughout the corporation from 70,000 to approximately 2,000.
- In the U.S. Air Force, the Air Force Occupational Measurement Squadron surveys every person in a particular occupational specialty to identify the skills used and not used in particular jobs. Based on this information, Air Force managers assess the content of specific training programs to eliminate irrelevant instruction from courses and ensure that graduates acquire the skills and knowledge they need to do their jobs.

A clear trend in all the systems considered in this study is the development of a learning organization of some sort that is responsible for more than just the assessment of existing providers. These organizations promote communications among stakeholders and develop a clear link between education and

# Ensuring Quality and Productivity in Higher Education

## An Analysis of Assessment Practices

Susan M. Gates, Catherine H. Augustine,
Roger Benjamin, Tora K. Bikson, Tessa Kaganoff,
Dina G. Levy, Joy S. Moini, Ron W. Zimmer

*ASHE-ERIC Higher Education Report: Volume 29, Number 1*
*Adrianna J. Kezar, Series Editor*

*Prepared and published by*

JOSSEY-BASS
A Wiley Company
San Francisco

*In cooperation with*

*ERIC Clearinghouse on Higher Education*
*The George Washington University*
*URL: www.eriche.org*

*Association for the Study*
*of Higher Education*
*URL: www.tiger.coe.missouri.edu/~ashe*

*Graduate School of Education and Human Development*
*The George Washington University*
*URL: www.gwu.edu*

**Ensuring Quality and Productivity in Higher Education: An Analysis of Assessment Practices**
Susan M. Gates, Catherine H. Augustine, Roger Benjamin, Tora K. Bikson,
Tessa Kaganoff, Dina G. Levy, Joy S. Moini, Ron W. Zimmer
ASHE-ERIC Higher Education Report: Volume 29, Number 1
Adrianna J. Kezar, Series Editor

This publication was prepared partially with funding from the Office of
Educational Research and Improvement, U.S. Department of Education, under
contract no. ED-99-00-0036. The opinions expressed in this report do not
necessarily reflect the positions or policies of OERI or the Department.

ISSN 0884-0040    electronic ISSN 1536-0709    ISBN 0-7879-5840-9

The ASHE-ERIC Higher Education Report is part of the Jossey-Bass Higher
and Adult Education Series and is published six times a year by Wiley Subscription
Services, Inc., a Wiley company, at Jossey-Bass, 989 Market Street, San Francisco,
California 94103-1741.

**For subscription information,** see the Back Issue/Subscription Order Form
in the back of this journal.

**Prospective authors** are strongly encouraged to contact Adrianna Kezar at
(301) 405-0868 or kezar@wam.umd.edu.

Visit the Jossey-Bass Web site at **www.josseybass.com.**

Printed in the United States of America on acid-free recycled paper.

professional development on the one hand and the basic mission of the system on the other. Corporate learning organizations describe this relationship as "becoming a strategic partner" in the corporation. Such an organization facilitates dialogue among key stakeholders, assembles information on workforce needs and existing programs, and serves as an interface between customers and providers.

## What Approaches Are Used to Assess Providers and Certify Students?

In reviewing a wide variety of assessment approaches, this study identified key similarities and differences among the approaches and classified them into four basic models. The first model involves the use of an intermediary organization that is responsible for reviewing the process used by individual providers to assess their own quality and productivity. In the second model, an intermediary organization conducts the actual assessment of providers. In the third model, providers conduct their own assessment with no involvement of an intermediary. The fourth model differs from the other three in that it focuses on the learner rather than the provider and involves the certification of student competencies. Each approach has strengths and weaknesses that make it more appropriate for some circumstances than for others. For that reason, no one approach can be considered a best practice. The best approach depends on the context of the assessment.

## How Does One Choose a Model?

Many organizations whose job is to ensure the quality and productivity of education and professional development activities can be described as *intermediary organizations*. An intermediary is neither a provider of education and professional development nor a direct consumer of the services of such providers; it is an entity that promotes communication between the two. Models One, Two, and Four, described in this report, allow a role for an intermediary and are therefore the most relevant to such entities. Intermediaries might also wish to learn about the best practices under Model Three, however, to serve as a clearinghouse of information useful to provider institutions and to remain abreast of new assessment techniques initiated by providers.

The study identified six factors as the most important to consider in choosing an approach to assessing the quality and productivity of providers: (1) purpose of the assessment (accountability versus improvement), (2) level of authority, (3) level of resources, (4) centralization of operations, (5) system heterogeneity, and (6) system complexity. We argue that Model One is particularly well suited to highly complex and decentralized systems. Model One is also most suitable for assessors who have little formal authority over providers and uncertain resources. This model is based on quality improvement concepts that have been used in the business world for the last twenty-five years and were adopted by the International Organization for Standardization (ISO) in the 1980s to promote high-quality standards among manufacturing companies. To qualify for this certification, an organization must define and document its quality standards for producing its goods or services in a policy document or quality manual that is reviewed by a third party.

The academic audit, a new approach to education assessment that has been influenced by the ISO, is another example of Model One. The audit is conducted by an intermediary organization and focuses on ensuring that providers of education have effective processes in place for measuring their own quality and thus can engage in ongoing self-improvement. Because this approach is more sensitive to the different missions and characteristics of institutions than are other approaches, it is particularly useful for systems with a diverse set of providers.

The key advantage of Model One is that it delegates to provider organizations the task of defining goals, measuring outcomes, and evaluating outcomes. As a result, this approach can accommodate a system with many diverse providers. Because they have such control over their own assessment, providers are less likely to resist the process and are more likely to use it to promote improvements.

The primary disadvantage of Model One relative to Model Two is that it emphasizes improvement over accountability. The trade-off between these two purposes of assessment remains an important issue for assessors. Model Two is better suited for accountability purposes, provided that the intermediary has the authority to ensure compliance. In Model Two, the intermediary sets the goals of the assessment, measures performance on these goals, and evaluates the performance. This model provides the intermediary with control of the assessment process suitable for accountability purposes. In these cases, the intermediary can focus on system-level goals, goals that the provider might otherwise ignore, to ensure that the provider is meeting the needs of the system. For example, many state legislatures mandate that higher education institutions provide data for "report cards" that grade institutions on how well they perform on goals such as graduation rates and contribution to the state's economic development. The main drawback to Model Two is that any approach imposed from an external organization runs the risk of focusing on inappropriate measures and failing to reflect institutional goals. In this case, providers may fail to comply with the request for information. Even in cases when providers do comply with requests for information, they may not internalize them or perform well on the goals set by the intermediaries. Thus, using Model Two does not necessarily result in institutional improvement.

Although Model Three is better suited for improvement, it does not include a role for an intermediary. Because Model Three is enacted by providers, its use is not constrained by system-level issues of complexity, authority, centralization, or heterogeneity. Despite the provider's control prescribed by Model Three, some of the most innovative examples of this model incorporate the perspectives of a range of stakeholders. In these cases, even though the provider is responsible for defining, measuring, and evaluating the attainment of its own goals, other stakeholders can be involved in these three steps. For example, administrators of the Urban Universities Portfolio Project use advisory boards comprising business leaders, government representatives, and educational experts to advise them on appropriate goals, indicators, and measures. In addition, intermediaries such as regional accrediting bodies are invited to use the resulting performance information in their assessment processes. Therefore, although Model Three is provider initiated, it can evolve into a process with a role for intermediaries.

Model Four represents a completely different approach to assessment, one that focuses attention on the learner rather than the provider. This competency-based approach can be used in assessment systems for both accountability and improvement purposes and may be similarly immune to system-level constraints such as complexity, authority, heterogeneity, and centralization. Although Model Four focuses on student competencies, it indirectly holds institutions accountable by withholding competency status from students who have not received the requisite education from specific providers. These providers must change to maintain their ability to attract students; in this way, the assessment process stimulates improvement while indirectly holding providers accountable for change. This approach is very attractive to employers and others who want to ascertain whether individuals have specific knowledge, skills, or abilities. This assessment can be time-consuming and expensive to carry out, however, especially if the competencies are abstract ones, such as critical thinking or problem solving. This approach may be therefore best suited for cases in which the knowledge required is easy to ascertain and assess, such as in training programs for specific occupations.

## What Is the Three-Step Process of Assessment?

Regardless of the model selected, the study found that three key steps must be included in any provider or student assessment:

- Identifying goals of the education activities under consideration
- Measuring the outcomes related to those goals
- Evaluating whether the outcomes meet those goals.

The literature review revealed several broad lessons concerning these steps. First, each step should be linked to the others, and the process as a whole should be driven by the goals. It is especially important to avoid selecting measures before or without defining goals. Practitioners in higher education, corporate, and government settings stress the tendency of people to value what is measured and focus exclusively on that information rather than linking what is measured to the purpose of the activity.

Second, developing measures that relate to goals is a crucial if difficult step. It is often difficult to find an adequate measure of achievement for a particular goal. It is usually better to use an imperfect measure of a specific goal than it is to use a perfect measure of something different, however. Engaging a broad range of stakeholders in this process helps to keep it focused on the goals of the undertaking. Such stakeholder involvement and continuous feedback is an explicit element of both the Baldrige Award process and the balanced scorecard.

Third, the trend in assessment is to focus less on input measures and more on process and outcome measures. Measuring outcomes alone may not result in improvement, but considering the intervening processes that use resources to produce outcomes provides information more useful to program improvement.

Finally, except for certificate or licensing programs, providers of professional development courses are not likely to be able to rely on preexisting evaluation tools with known validity and reliability characteristics. Rather, they will most likely have to develop measures of learning outcomes on their own. The literature provides some guidelines for developing such measures and for avoiding major sources of invalidity and unreliability. Intermediaries can play an important role by applying these guidelines to their own assessment processes and acting as clearinghouses of such information for providers engaged in assessment.

# Contents

# Foreword

Each week the *Chronicle of Higher Education* is filled with stories about legislators' and the public's concern about the cost and quality of higher education
and the need for the system to respond to more problems of greater complexity, such as the need to resolve international tensions around globaliza-
tion. In response to these calls for change, many new systems—report cards,
a national study of student engagement, assessment, institutional research, and
the like—purport to aid higher education in examining its structures
and processes. In the last decade, leaders in higher education have come to
realize that assessment or some new forms of accountability and improvement
are likely to become part of the enterprise. Faculty, administrators, and even
students are aware of the pressures to be accountable and to improve higher
education. But how do we make sense of all these newly developed mechanisms? Which ones work and how do they work? Although this monograph
does not review all these systems, it provides a framework to examine and evaluate these various approaches to accountability and improvement.

The ASHE-ERIC Higher Education Reports have long been committed
to understanding and presenting the best research on assessment. This
monograph emerged out of an extensive national project conducted by
RAND. It is another expression of this long-standing commitment. Susan
Gates, Catherine Augustine, and Tessa Kaganoff provide guidance on system-
level assessment, which will be invaluable to legislators, trustees, governing
boards, state systems, accreditors, and other individuals and groups entrusted
to ensure the vitality of higher education. The monograph is also an important contribution because it examines our assumptions about assessment. Most

assessment efforts focus on accountability and pay only lip service to improvement. Is society willing to spend the time and money to develop extensive assessment practices that do not run deeper than merely understanding whether higher education is meeting its commitment to society? It seems critical to focus on how assessment can be used for improvement and to design systems that are effective in meeting this goal. I applaud the authors for not only asking the hard questions (such as why goals and methods are often unaligned) but also developing constructive solutions. It is easy to say system-level assessment does not work as well as it should, but it is difficult to develop practical and implementable ideas for improving it.

The monograph includes a focused literature review as well as a discussion of research results from a national study. Although the literature synthesizes concepts about system-level assessment, it has implications for assessment at all levels, especially around issues of alignment of goals and design. The authors' work uncovers important principles for advancing our assessment practices, such as the need to more clearly identify the goals of the process up front, choose appropriate measures, and use those measures to evaluate progress toward those goals.

Several other ASHE-ERIC Reports are important supplements for this monograph. Gaither, Nedweck, and Neal, in their monograph *Measuring Up,* focus specifically on performance indicators as a method of accountability among state systems. Alstete reviews approaches to benchmarking, a particular method of assessment used by many campuses for improvement across the institution in programs, departments, schools, and colleges, whereas Creamer examines assessment for a particular group (faculty) in her monograph *Assessing Faculty Publication Productivity.* Each monograph reviews different aspects of assessment that can be used for advancing campus efforts related to improvement and accountability.

**Adrianna J. Kezar**
ASHE-ERIC Series Editor
University of Maryland

# Introduction

R EADERS OF THE higher education literature and practitioners in the field are aware of the web of accountability arrangements in which colleges and universities exist today. Various constituents, including students, parents, government officials, and employers, have suggested one method or another for holding higher education institutions accountable (Banta, 1988; Banta and Borden, 1994; Boyer, Ewell, Finney, and Mingle, 1987; Council for Higher Education Accreditation, 2000; Ruppert, 1995; Schulz, 1996). The end result of these demands is a complex array of assessors, including accrediting agencies, state higher education boards, professional societies, and individual customers (Albright, 1995; Ewell, 1987b; Ewell, 1993; Ewell, 1999b; Lenth, 1996; Stevens and Hamlett, 1983). This phenomenon is not unique to higher education; demands for accountability have also increased in the federal government. In the 1990s, Congress passed several pieces of legislation, including the Government Performance and Results Act (GPRA) of 1993, that address waste and inefficiency, increase program effectiveness, and improve the internal management of the federal government. The GPRA directs the 24 largest federal agencies to submit five-year strategic plans as well as annual performance plans with their budget requests to Congress (Office of Management and Budget, 1998).

Although researchers have devoted substantial attention to how providers of postsecondary education respond to these calls for accountability and how the system might change as a result, little attention has been devoted to understanding the role of those entities responsible for ensuring accountability. What do they do? How is what they do different from the role of other assessors?

What is the impact of their activities? It is important to consider the roles, objectives, and behavior of these assessors so that new entrants to the assessment field can learn from their experiences and not duplicate their efforts and so that all assessors understand the constellation of forces acting upon individual providers (Ewell and Wellman, 1997; Western Association of Schools and Colleges, 1998, 1999).

Most of the current body of research on assessment focuses on the institution and issues internal to the institution. For example, the ASHE-ERIC Higher Education series has explored methods for structuring assessment to minimize the likelihood of faculty resistance, ways institutions can utilize benchmarking to measure and improve performance, ways Continuous Quality Improvement has been used by different institutions, and different techniques for improving the quality of student outcomes (Alstete, 1995; Gardiner, 1994; Schilling and Schilling, 1998; Wolverton, 1994). This document complements the existing literature by focusing on assessors and the approaches they use to accomplish their objectives. In so doing, it considers the potential assessment role of all stakeholders in a system of education.

**This document complements the existing literature by focusing on assessors and the approaches they use to accomplish their objectives.**

An education system consists of customers of education, providers of education, and intermediary organizations that mediate, oversee, or assess educational services. All of them are stakeholders within the system who have an interest in the educational services provided, and all may play a role in assessment. There are also stakeholders outside the system itself, who might provide funding for the education system or stand to benefit from its services or both (see Easton, 1965).

Intermediaries are organizations that mediate between customers and providers and provide a locus for the consideration of system-level issues.[1] Potential roles for an intermediary include:

- Assessing quality and productivity
- Providing useful information and guidance to customers and/or providers

- Helping to aggregate the demands of many customers
- Helping to resolve disagreements among different levels of customers or between customers and providers
- Leading systemwide planning efforts
- Providing incentives for change at the provider level.

Examples of intermediaries are state higher education planning boards, professional societies, and corporate learning organizations.

This study examines the roles of assessors in higher education and professional development settings, be they providers, customers, or intermediaries in the education system. The findings are based on a broad review of how educational quality and productivity are assessed in a variety of settings. We found that a number of very different activities are described in terms of "assessment of education and professional development." As a result, a large part of the effort that went into this report involved defining terms and creating a structure for talking about the different elements of assessment used in different sectors. We are aware of no other report that brings together lessons on assessment from such a wide variety of organizations and believe that this document will prove useful to those interested in the assessment of colleges and universities, state higher education systems, corporations, and government agencies.

The role of ensuring accountability is a challenging one under most circumstances, but the complexity is compounded when the assessment covers an entire system, such as a state, as well as individual provider institutions within the system. Systems often assign the task of ensuring system-level accountability to intermediaries, such as to state coordinating boards or to the centralized learning organizations found in corporate universities (National Center for Higher Education Management Systems, 1996; Meister, 1998). These intermediaries frequently focus their attention on assessing the quality and productivity of the providers within their system, essentially assuming that system-level accountability will follow from provider accountability. Many intermediaries tackle provider assessment through an approach similar to that of accreditation or licensing. Although we address such models in this monograph, we also introduce alternative approaches to assessment that may be more appropriate for an intermediary, depending on the context. These models and the relevant context factors are examined in detail to help intermediaries make assessment choices.

Although this report considers assessment by customers, providers, and intermediaries, much of our work focuses attention on the perspective of the intermediary. We include examples to illustrate the unique challenges facing specific intermediaries. Our primary intention with these examples is to point out the generalities in the approaches taken and challenges facing intermediaries; however, we acknowledge that there are considerable differences in the problems confronting different types of intermediaries. For example, many state boards of higher education are faced with overseeing highly autonomous institutions (including private sector institutions in some cases). Such high autonomy presents challenges that may not be present in corporate sectors and federal agencies. Although we do not go into great detail about some of these important differences among sectors in the main body of this report, we hope that the examples will provide greater detail on how specific intermediaries handle the challenges unique to their sector and industry.

## Objectives and Approach

Our research is based on a review of the literature on quality and productivity in education and professional development activities and of the methods used by various organizations that assess quality and productivity. The analysis was supplemented by interviews with experts on quality and productivity assessment, attendance at conferences on quality and productivity assessment, and site visits to organizations responsible for assessing quality and productivity.

The literature on this topic falls into two categories. The first includes theoretical literature on quality and productivity and offers general frameworks for assessment, including accreditation, program review, academic audit, and such business-based methods as the balanced scorecard, the Baldrige criteria, ISO 9000,[2] and benchmarking. We reviewed a broad range of sources, including journal articles, published reports or manuals, and Web sites.

Because the theoretical literature is so voluminous, we chose to focus on an objectives-oriented approach for evaluating quality and productivity.

Although other approaches are less common, some researchers have focused on internal organizational processes in defining effectiveness (see, e.g., Steers, 1975), and others have adapted a system resource model (e.g., Yuchtman and Seashore, 1967) in which organizational effectiveness is defined as the ability of the organization to exploit its environment to acquire optimal amounts of scarce and valuable resources. Despite these other efforts, the objectives-oriented approach is the dominant trend in higher education, business, and government. The GPRA, for example, mandates that government programs be evaluated and justified on the basis of their contribution to the performance objectives of the government agencies responsible for them. An objectives-oriented approach often includes other considerations (e.g., it might include a consumer-oriented approach to the extent that consumer demand is taken as an indicator of the quality of the program delivered).

The other body of literature on quality and productivity assessment describes the actual practices of organizations that are assessing the quality and/or productivity of education and training services. Our review of this literature focused on new developments and "best practices" used for quality and productivity assessment. In some areas, the existing literature included comprehensive reviews, comparisons, and evaluations of the assessment practices. Such literature existed mainly for institutions of higher education and corporate universities. In reviewing the quality and productivity assessment activities of other types of organizations, we had to rely mainly on primary source documents (e.g., reports, Web sites).

In addition to the literature review, we conducted phone and in-person interviews with representatives of organizations responsible for assessing academic quality and productivity as well as with experts in the field of academic quality and productivity assessment. Through the course of the literature review and the interviews, we identified a comprehensive list of assessment approaches. In selecting specific approaches and organizations to profile in the report, we used several criteria. First, we wanted breadth, so we profiled examples of every approach we identified, including approaches from different sectors (such as corporate universities and education and training in the context of a federal agency). Within each sector, we selected specific organizations to profile based on the extent to which information was available about the assessment approaches used. In the cases of the innovative approaches, there was usually only one organization associated with the approach, such as with the Baldrige Award or the Urban Universities Portfolio Project. For more widely used approaches, we profiled three types of organizations: (1) innovative users of the approach (e.g., Western Association of Schools and Colleges [WASC]); (2) organizations that seem to typify the approach (e.g., *US News & World Report*); or (3) examples that people working in the assessment field identified as "best practices" (e.g., Kentucky Council on Postsecondary Education or Lucent Technologies).

In addition to the literature review, we conducted phone interviews and site visits to a subset of the profiled cases. The main document synthesizes the literature review and draws lessons from the interviews and site visits. In spite of the wide variety of organizations reviewed, we were able to identify key similarities across approaches. These similarities provided a foundation for a categorization scheme that provides a structure for this report.

# Framework

The framework we present reflects our attempt to bring together insights from a wide array of assessment activities through a common conceptual structure. This structure helps to identify similarities and differences across assessment approaches. To accomplish this goal, we must convey to the reader a set of definitions that are used throughout the report.

Following the comprehensive review of the higher education assessment literature in Palomba and Banta (1999), we use the word *assessment* to refer to the multistep process of examining the quality and productivity of education and professional development activities. We use the word *evaluation* to describe the step in the assessment process in which measures of quality and productivity are examined against some standard of performance. And we use the word *productivity* to mean the level and quality of service obtained from a given amount of resources (Epstein, 1992). In this sense, it is synonymous with efficiency. If the provider of education can produce a greater quantity or a higher quality of service with the same level of resources, it has improved its productivity or efficiency (Houston, 1992). *Quality* is used interchangeably with *effectiveness*. There is no single definition of quality: it means different things to different people. In an assessment process, the meaning of quality typically emerges through the process of identifying goals for the assessment. The quality or effectiveness of an education system is defined in terms of performance as required by multiple stakeholders, including students, employers, parents, accreditors, and the government (McGuinness, 1997). In this sense, quality is in the eye of the beholder. As can be seen by these definitions, the concept of productivity includes a consideration of quality so that improvement in productivity is not synonymous with cost cutting (Schapiro, 1993; Gilmore and To, 1992; Albright, 1995). Both quality and productivity are thus multifaceted concepts, inextricably linked with the goals and missions of the system, institution, and stakeholders.

**In an assessment process, the meaning of quality typically emerges through the process of identifying goals for the assessment.**

Assessment of the quality and productivity of vast systems of education is a complex and multidimensional process. Our analysis of the process, as well as the organization of this report, rests on several important distinctions concerning the level of assessment, the approach to assessment, and the steps of the assessment process.

Our analysis suggests that any assessment of system performance embodies two distinct levels of activity: the system level and the provider level. Much of the literature on assessment in higher education and corporations emphasizes provider-level assessment (e.g., Massy, 1994; Palomba and Banta, 1999; Ruppert, 1995). Our review of specific organizations highlights the importance of assessment that takes place at the system level, however (see Meister, 1998). That type of assessment, which we call *Phase One,* poses two questions that cannot be answered by assessing individual providers: (1) Are the needs of all potential customers being acknowledged by the system? and (2) Are system-level objectives being addressed by providers? Provider-level assessment, which we call *Phase Two,* evaluates how well individual providers of education are meeting the needs of their customers. Because it extends beyond the boundaries of any one institution, the system-level assessment of Phase One can be carried out only by an intermediary organization that operates outside provider institutions. Phase Two assessment can be conducted by customers, providers, or intermediaries. Phase One assessment is crucial to accountability, because it deals with the issue of whether there is a mismatch between what providers are doing and what the system needs. Recent research in the higher education sector confirms this stance. After conducting empirical case studies of five states, Richardson, Bracco, Callan, and Finney (1998) concluded that states need to define their expectations of providers, assess how well providers' performance is meeting these expectations, and find solutions for existing gaps between performance and expectations. This scenario is applicable for corporations and government agencies as well. A provider that delivers very high quality education in an area that is of no use to the system is ultimately not accountable to the system. We found that many educational assessment activities simply overlook Phase One and therefore fail to discern systemic problems. Intermediary organizations can play an important role in Phase One assessment, because they are more likely than providers to consider the needs of many stakeholders. It remains challenging, however, for a single intermediary organization to internalize the needs of the whole system.

For Phase Two assessment of provider institutions, we identified four main approaches to assessment that differ along several dimensions (see "Phase Two: Assessing How Well Providers Meet Customers' Needs"). Three of the approaches, which we call *Models One, Two, and Three,* focus on assessing the performance of the provider. *Model Four* focuses on assessing the competencies of the student. The models are further distinguished by such factors as who designs and carries out the assessment process and the process's primary purpose.

Regardless of what approach is taken to assess providers, our review of the literature and case studies found that there are basically three steps in the process, each with its own important requirements (see Palomba and Banta, 1999, for a comprehensive overview of the assessment process in higher education):

- *Identify* the goals of education or professional development.
- *Measure performance:* Identify and implement measures of performance.

- *Evaluate* the extent to which the performance measures meet the education and professional development goals.

The first step, identifying goals, is often overlooked in system assessments. When assessors go right to the second task of defining measures of performance without first identifying goals, they run the danger of committing themselves to measuring outcomes that do not clearly relate to the objectives of the education system. They may either develop extraneous measures or neglect measures that reflect core system objectives. In the first instance, time will be wasted collecting and analyzing irrelevant information. In the second instance, they will not know whether the system is meeting important objectives.

# Organization of the Report

This document draws together the results of our broad review of literature and practice and highlights important themes, lessons, and best practices of potential interest to those responsible for assessing education and professional development activities. The next chapter, "Phase One: System-Level Assessment," provides a more detailed description of the system-level assessment of Phase One. "Phase Two: Assessing How Well Providers Meet Customers' Needs" compares the four main models to assessing quality and productivity in Phase Two, including their relative strengths and limitations. "Choosing the Right Model for Phase Two" discusses the factors that are most important to consider in deciding on an appropriate model for assessment. "Three Steps for Assessing Providers" describes the three steps involved in any assessment process: (1) defining goals of the system, (2) choosing appropriate measures, and (3) using those measures to evaluate progress toward those goals. The final chapter, "Conclusions and Recommendations," offers some final observations designed to guide those engaged in assessment.

# Phase One: System-Level Assessment

THE ASSESSMENT OF ANY education system involves more than assessing individual providers of that education. Our case studies reveal the importance of a higher-level assessment that addresses issues beyond individual institutions, such as whether the network of providers is reaching all potential customers, whether it is meeting the needs of the system as a whole, and whether the system itself, rather than any individual provider or customer, is allocating its resources efficiently. System-level assessment of this kind has not received much treatment in the literature. As a result, our description of Phase One assessment drew largely on case studies of state higher education systems such as the state of Texas, corporations such as Lucent Technologies, and military services and government agencies such as the U.S. Department of Transportation's system of education and professional development.

> **The assessment of any education system involves more than assessing individual providers of that education.**

## Goals of System-Level Assessment

System-level assessment has two main goals. One is to detect any misalignments between customers' needs, system-level needs, and providers' offerings. The other is to determine whether the system's resources are being allocated in a way that will optimize their effects. Each objective poses its own challenges.

### *Identifying Misalignment*

Misalignments can come in various forms. For example, system-level assessment should address whether all potential customers are being reached by the services provided. In a state higher education system, certain geographical regions of a state may be underserved by the existing set of institutions. In a corporation or government agency, the needs of certain lines of business might be ignored by existing programs.

In other cases, the customer that is not being well served may be at a higher level of the hierarchy of customers. For example, the lines of business in a corporation might have narrower training objectives than the corporate officers, who might be interested in building a corporate culture or other more general training. In corporations where training and education are the responsibility of individual business units, no single business unit may want to take responsibility for corporate leadership training.

Another type of misalignment in the system is that the network of providers may not fully support the system's overall mission. In other words, educational services may be offered that have nothing to do with carrying out the organization's goals.[3] At Lucent Technologies, for example, educational activities are provided with one purpose in mind: to help the company achieve growth in key markets. If a program or course cannot be linked to this objective, Lucent does not offer it.

This focus on mission-driven education and professional development can also be found in public sector organizations, such as the U.S. Department of Transportation (DOT). The goal of the DOT Learning and Development Program is to "enhance the operation of the Department in accomplishing its mission by investing in the development and utilization of its human resources" (U.S. Department of Transportation, 1997a). This goal is linked to DOT's overall management strategy, "ONE DOT," which is designed to develop an integrated and unified department to provide the highest-quality transportation system for the country. The Learning and Development Program sees a clear need for partnership with managers of the operating administrations that control key business areas in designing and assessing training.

*Optimizing Resource Allocation at the System Level*

All the education systems we studied dealt with limited resources. Many of the education systems are embedded within larger systems (e.g., corporations, government agencies, or states) that had primary missions other than education, training, and professional development. As a result, the leaders of the larger system had to determine how to allocate education and training resources efficiently and effectively. This is the crux of the system-level productivity issue: Are the system's resources being allocated in such a way as to maximize their impact? Our case studies illustrate the ways in which different systems address this issue. This issue has also been addressed in the literature in descriptions of systems struggling to effectively allocate their resources (Phillips, 1997; Mann, 1996–97; Joint Staff for the Committee, 1957; Cavalluzzo and Cymrot, 1998; Benjamin and others, 2000).

# How Systems Establish a Structure for Such Assessment

To carry out such high-level assessment, most large systems set up an entity responsible for looking at the "big picture" education and professional development issues that can be assessed only at the system level. This entity is neither a direct customer nor a provider, but an intermediary. In states, that entity is a state higher education board; in corporations, military services, and government agencies, it is a central learning organization of some type.

As our case studies showed, these intermediaries must be closely tied to the customers and providers. Although the education systems we reviewed differ in profound ways, those that were engaged in system-level assessment were surprisingly consistent on this point: they were able to operate at a strategic level because they had high-level involvement from system leaders—such as the state governor, the CEO, or the secretary of the military service—and they were fully integrated into the operating units of the organization in which they were embedded or the institutions over which they had oversight. This integration provides access to regular information on the priorities and needs of the overall system of which they are a part.

Several case studies provide examples of such integration:

- In Kentucky, the governor has made higher education a defining issue of his administration and played a key role in reshaping the Kentucky Council on Postsecondary Education (CPE). There is also a Strategic Committee on Postsecondary Education (SCOPE), which includes the governor, the state general assembly leadership, and the leadership of CPE. The purpose of SCOPE is to ensure that the elected leaders play a role in developing the strategic agenda for postsecondary education.
- In the corporate environment, central learning organizations headed by a "chief learning officer" are replacing a model in which training was controlled by individual lines of business, each of which had its own training activities to meet its specific needs. This shift to more centralized planning is similar to the transition that information technology went through in the 1980s, when the term *chief information officer* was relatively new. Corporate learning organizations have recognized the importance of getting buy-in from both the company's chief executive officer and the heads of lines of business in support of their efforts.
- In the Air Force education and training establishment, many stakeholders are involved at different stages of the process: commanders at different levels identify training requirements and priorities; Air Education and Training Command is the primary agency responsible for training development and assessment; major commands identify mission demands and training/personnel needs; Air Force deputy chiefs of staff oversee the management and policies for training. They, along with the training managers, supervisors, and students, provide input into the quality assessment process.
- The U.S. Department of Transportation education and professional development process is coordinated through the Learning and Development Program in the Office of Human Resource Management. Collaboration is continuous between this program and the operating administrations of DOT. Members of the human resources department of every operating administration sit on the Learning and Development Council and provide input and feedback on education and development policies for the department as a whole.

- Lucent Technologies established a structure for systemwide assessment by creating business performance councils that support curricula in fifteen different areas, such as software, wireless, diversity, and program management. Each business performance council comprises powerful people in the company. For example, the software committee is led by the vice president for software. More than 160 people sit on these councils. There is a dean for each curriculum, and about twenty subject matter experts help with curriculum design. The success of the business performance councils and of the learning and development activities in general is driven by several factors, including strong, executive-level leadership and support and broad involvement with the business units. The councils are responsible for much more than education and training, highlighting the link between education and professional development and corporate goals. They consider all strategic issues related to the particular subject area.

Such integrated learning organizations are well suited to the tasks of Phase One assessment.

## How Systems Identify Misalignments

One of the goals of Phase One assessment is to identify the gaps between what is needed and what is provided, determine which gaps can and should be addressed by learning solutions, and develop learning solutions to help close those gaps. As a practical matter, however, the first step in that process—often referred to as *needs analysis*—is difficult to accomplish.

The most structured approach to needs analysis we observed was in the Air Force. The Air Force uses the Instructional System Development model to determine what instruction is and is not needed. This step is conducted by the Air Force Occupational Measurement Squadron (AFOMS), which surveys every person in a particular occupational specialty to determine the skills that are used (and not used) in different jobs.[4] The activities of AFOMS provide the information necessary for Air Force managers to determine whether the appropriate training needs are being addressed. They do not address individual job performance or the quality of the training provided. That work is done by staff at the training centers. AFOMS focuses exclusively on collecting data about the work done in each specialty in every career field and comparing that with information on the training being provided by the Air Force. AFOMS reports become the departure point for decision making on key issues, including skills that are being trained but not used in the Air Force and skills that are used but not trained.

Lucent Technologies has also recognized the importance of this type of needs analysis, and the different business performance councils are at different stages in the development of tools for identifying competency gaps. At this point, only two of the councils (software and program management) have a strong needs analysis methodology in place. The software council uses an industry-wide tool called the Kiviat. The Kiviat is a measurement tool that helps assess proficiencies and identify gaps in eight software project areas: customer focus, project management, project team variables, tools, quality focus, methodologies, physical environment, and metrics. The tool includes a detailed instrument, with twenty metrics in each area, for measuring a company's performance relative to others in the industry on a five-point scale. The performance measures are evaluated on the basis of ten years of industry-wide data. The software council uses the results of the Kiviat to point out areas where Lucent's performance is not leading edge and then considers whether learning solutions might be able to help improve performance in these areas.

The two state higher education coordinating boards that we reviewed had a much less structured approach to needs analysis at the system level. Often, gaps between needs and offerings are identified when some constituency group is motivated to complain about the current offerings. In the 1990s, for example, forty-eight counties filed a lawsuit against the state of Texas because they felt that the region was not being provided with enough educational opportunities. This lawsuit led to growth in higher education spending in that region of the state. In addition, the state of Texas recently commissioned a study by the Council for Aid to Education to help identify state higher education needs through demographic and labor market analyses (Benjamin and others, 2000).

# How Systems Allocate Resources

There are two ways to think about the allocation of resources. At the highest level, the system allocates resources for assessment. Then, within each system, the results of an assessment can affect the allocation of resources. We saw variation across both these dimensions in the systems we studied. As an example, at the state level, state legislators and governors appropriate money to coordinating and governing boards. These boards have multiple responsibilities, including assessment—how much of their budget gets spent on assessment is determined by the board—with input from their advisory boards. Assessment results can then impact the distribution of state funding for higher education, as in the case of state performance funding systems (Banta, 1988; Hebel, 1999; Stein and Fajen, 1995).

Corporate universities approach resource allocation in two different ways: (1) "pay for services" and (2) allocating funds out of corporate overhead (Meister, 1998). In the "pay for services" model, an open market system determines the number and type of courses offered. In this way, the quality of courses is assessed through customer demand: business units will not send staff to classes that they deem poor quality or not relevant. In the overhead model, a central office determines the number and type of classes and conducts assessment as well. Lucent, as described below, is a good example of this second model.

Of all our case studies, Lucent Technologies has the most impressive record of improving the productivity of its education and professional development system. Since 1995, the Lucent Learning Performance Center has increased the total number of learner days by more than 60 percent and decreased the cost per learner day by about 50 percent. It achieved these results by taking several steps:

- Reducing redundancies in course development and design. For example, about 700 courses on fire extinguisher operation were offered. This process allowed Lucent to consolidate about 70,000 courses offered to about 2,000 courses.
- Decreasing the number of vendors from which courses were purchased.

- Improving the focus of the courses Lucent developed internally, thereby reducing the number of those courses from 800 to 390.
- Reducing the number of staff sent to high-cost programs, such as the Wharton School of Business Executive MBA Program, whose value did not justify their cost.
- Increasing the use of Web-based instruction to reduce travel costs.

Compared with the Lucent Learning Performance Center or the DOT Learning and Development Program, the Texas Higher Education Coordinating Board has much less control over what education offerings are provided by the public institutions in the state. This board does exert some influence, however, through its authority to approve programs as eligible for state funding. In exercising that authority, it also considers whether existing offerings are meeting state needs and whether they do so efficiently.

The Texas Higher Education Coordinating Board's strategic plan (1999–2003) emphasizes that one of the board's key functions is "to eliminate costly duplication in academic programs and technical programs." This goal is accomplished through a review process that is based on five criteria: need (does the state need this program at this particular institution?), quality, cost, duplication (would a proposed program duplicate existing programs within the geographic area?), and mission (does the program fall within the institution's mission?). In spite of these reviews, the staff of the board know that they will not be able to identify all the programs that should be eliminated (they maintain that approximately 10 percent will be bad investments). The key is to establish a process of ongoing review so that the number of ineffective programs can be continually reduced.

The Air Force Air Education and Training Command (AETC) uses the instructional system development (ISD) process in developing its training programs. "The goal of ISD is to increase the effectiveness and cost efficiency of education by developing instruction on job performance requirements, eliminating irrelevant skills and knowledge instruction from courses, and ensuring that graduates acquire the necessary skills and knowledge to do the job" (U.S. Department of the Air Force, 2000). As a result, "ISD is a total quality process" that provides a system approach to training (U.S. Department of the

Air Force, 1993). Similarly, in the Navy, the primary goals of education and training assessment are to provide more training to more sailors at lower cost and to provide sailors the skills they need to do the job.

## Need for Standardized Data and Course Offerings

In many systems we examined, education and professional development activities emerged over time in a decentralized manner on an as-needed basis (Meister, 1998; Education Commission of the States, 1997). No centralized entity coordinated and monitored that growth and development. By the time many of these systems realized the potential value of Phase One assessment, the information required to conduct such an assessment was highly decentralized and difficult to assemble. Thus, an important task for many entities responsible for Phase One assessment has been gathering comparable data on providers so that intermediaries can make comparisons among providers and decisions about such providers. Sophisticated management information systems have made this task easier (Richardson and others, 1999).

**An important task for many entities responsible for Phase One assessment has been gathering comparable data on providers so that intermediaries can make comparisons among providers and decisions about such providers.**

For example, the Texas Higher Education Coordinating Board developed a workforce education course manual, a statewide inventory of courses offered by technical and community colleges (Texas Higher Education Coordinating Board, 2000). The creation of the manual was motivated in part by complaints from state residents about the difficulty of transferring credits among different institutions in the state and in part by the recognition that there was excessive program duplication. To develop the manual, the Texas board gathered experts and faculty together and got them to agree on a set of courses, appropriate content descriptions, and an appropriate range of contact hours for courses in particular course sequences. In welding, for example, they reduced the number of courses from 900 to 96. Overall, they went from more than 30,000 courses to about 6,000. Now, introductory welding has the same course name at every college offering it, and the course involves the same number of total contact hours, regardless of where it is delivered. A person could take the course in Del Rio and then be ready to take the next course in the sequence in San Antonio. Developing the manual took about four years and cost approximately $150,000 per year.

An added benefit of the effort to produce the manual is that it facilitates data gathering and tracking of students. As part of the ongoing review of two-year colleges, the coordinating board has developed the Academic Performance Indicator System. The information system contains longitudinal data on courses and students (demographic information, Social Security number, what courses they are taking, and graduation and Texas employment status). Students can be tracked across colleges and into the workforce by linking Social Security numbers to Texas workforce commission data. This tracking capability and the ability to track student, course, and college performance in one system is greatly facilitated by having the manual. This data effort costs approximately $530,000 annually.

## Beyond Assessment: Promoting Workforce Improvement

Phase One efforts create a structure for identifying system needs on an ongoing basis. Some of these efforts go well beyond assessment. Centralized learning organizations, for example, provide a range of services that are ultimately designed to promote workforce or even corporate improvement (Meister, 1998; Holton, 1996; Gray, McKenzie, Miller, and Shasky, 1997; Bassi, 2000; Bassi and Van Buren, 1999). They help employees develop individual learning plans to meet their training needs and keep track of their training accomplishments. The consolidation of courses at Lucent Technologies has made it easier to integrate training records with personnel records. Formerly, Lucent kept training records on employees, but they were not centralized, thus making it difficult to construct a training history on an individual. Now, if a learner successfully completes a course, it is noted in the person's record. In addition, the system allows students to search for and enroll in courses on-line.

Some learning organizations, such as the one at Sun Microsystems, have introduced information "portals" that organize information functionally, allowing employees to easily find what they need about learning opportunities throughout the company. United Airlines is also developing an interactive Web site that includes on-line tests that help an employee determine the skills (math, verbal, and leadership) he or she is lacking. The Web site is a huge information clearinghouse, organized on the basis of the tests and other information for the benefit of the user. For example, the learner can pull up a list of learning opportunities, both internal and external, that are available through United. Using well developed Web tools, learning organizations can connect and coordinate learning experiences for employees.

## Multiple Benefits

The process of determining whether the system is addressing the needs of the system as a whole can have many important benefits:

- It identifies where additional education and professional development are needed, as well as where redundancies have developed.
- It ties education and professional development to the primary mission of the system.
- It encourages prioritizing among competing needs.

# Phase Two: Assessing How Well Providers Meet Customers' Needs

PHASE TWO OF THE ASSESSMENT of education systems focuses on the performance of specific providers of educational services. Although such assessment is sometimes driven by system-level goals, the unit of analysis for assessment is either a provider organization or the student. This section describes the main approaches used to conduct such assessments. As with the rest of this report, this section summarizes and draws key lessons from assessment approaches used in a wide variety of contexts. Although all of the literature we reviewed and all of our case studies concerned assessment, we found that each assessment organization (e.g., accrediting agencies, corporate learning organizations) uses a different language to describe what it does. This section summarizes the diverse set of assessment approaches, describing models of assessment that capture the key differences among approaches.

We identified four models for determining how well providers are meeting the needs of their customers. The models distill the key characteristics that distinguish the approaches from one another (see Figure 1). In the first model, the provider conducts the assessment of education activities, and an intermediary institution reviews the process used by the provider to conduct its self-assessment. In Model One, the intermediary does not establish goals against which the provider should be evaluated or actually evaluate whether the provider is good or bad. Instead, the intermediary focuses on whether the provider has done a proper self-assessment. This approach is similar to an accounting audit in which the accounting firm verifies that a company has followed the proper accounting rules in maintaining its books but does not comment on whether the company is financially healthy. In

**FIGURE 1**
**Four Models for Assessing Providers**

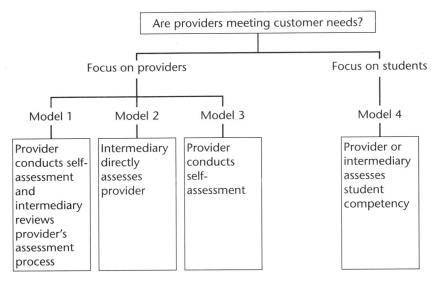

Model Two, on the other hand, the intermediary actually conducts the assessment: it defines assessment goals, designs the assessment process, and evaluates institutional performance based on data from the provider. Model Three differs from both these models in that there is no role for an intermediary: the provider acts independently in conducting its self-assessment. With this approach, customers have no third party to verify the accuracy or reliability of the provider's self-assessment as in Model One. In the fourth model, either the provider or an intermediary also conducts the assessment, but in this case the focus is on student competencies. The assumption behind this approach is that measuring what students have learned is the best way to assess performance of the education system as a whole.[5]

# Model One: Intermediary Assesses or Guides Provider's Process of Assessment

What is unique about Model One is that an intermediary organization is responsible for overseeing the assessment process used by provider institutions. This approach, which has its origins in the business world, is receiving growing interest in the education community because it allows education institutions to develop their own assessment processes that best reflect their education and training goals. In reviewing these processes, the intermediary organization focuses on whether the goals are reasonable and whether the measures are valid and reliable indicators of the achievement of the goals. Because this approach does not typically impose goals from the outside, each provider may be assessed against different goals.

One of the best examples of this approach is outside the education community: the International Organization for Standardization process quality standards, called ISO 9000. The clearest example of Model One in the academic world is the academic audit, an approach developed outside the United States that is only now attracting wide attention in this country.

**Model One . . . , which has its origins in the business world, is receiving growing interest in the education community because it allows education institutions to develop their own assessment processes that best reflect their education and training goals.**

## *ISO 9000*

ISO 9000 certification is a widely recognized and highly regarded stamp of approval for manufacturing companies. Developed in the late 1980s, it was designed to provide quality standards of production worldwide and thereby facilitate business deals between producers and consumers. To achieve ISO 9000 certification, leaders of an organization must explicitly define and document their policy for quality, which ultimately becomes a *quality manual.* The adopted policy should be not only a standard of quality within the organization but also a standard of quality that can be verified and certified by a third party. The ISO 9000 process also requires that measures be developed for assessing a process and that the leaders of the organization explicitly define the quality standards for producing products or services. The organizational standards should be stated principally in terms of performance. Because evaluation is an essential part of the ISO 9000 philosophy, it is crucial that workers keep up-to-date documentation that external auditors can use to certify (or register) the organization as an ISO organization. ISO registration does not guarantee that an organization's products are of high quality, but it serves as evidence that the organization is strictly adhering to its own internal quality production standards. The customer must decide for itself whether the quality standards are good enough to guarantee a product of high enough quality from its perspective. To become certified, a third-party organization must serve as an objective evaluator of the organization's adherence to its quality manual. In theory, once an organization is certified, it is recognized around the world as having a quality system that is fully and consistently used. The certification lasts for three years.

Recently, the ISO developed a new set of standards and guidelines that could be applied to service industries, including education. Some researchers argue that the ISO 9000, along with total quality management strategies, can be used in an education context to enhance customer satisfaction, reduce student attrition, and improve graduation rates while reducing costs (Vandenberge, 1995; Spanbauer, 1992). But the academic community has shown substantial resistance to this approach, partly because of its reluctance to adopt strategies from the business world.

### The Academic Audit

The purpose of an academic audit is to ensure that institutions have processes in place for measuring their own quality and thus can engage in ongoing self-improvement (see Appendix B). A relatively new approach to quality assessment has been implemented abroad—in Hong Kong, Scandinavia, Great Britain, Australia, New Zealand, and the Association of European Universities—and is beginning to receive attention in the United States, particularly from certain regional accrediting organizations. It has been influenced by the process-oriented quality assessment tradition in the private sector such as total quality management and the ISO 9000, but it is less adversarial and more collaborative and is therefore viewed by academics as less alien than many techniques used in the business world.

**The purpose of an academic audit is to ensure that institutions have processes in place for measuring their own quality and thus can engage in ongoing self-improvement.**

Academic audits are normally conducted by an external organization or intermediary, but that organization often brings together representatives of provider institutions and other stakeholders as well. In Hong Kong, for example, the audits are carried out by the University Grants Committee, a large advisory body including distinguished overseas academics, prominent local professionals and businesspeople, and senior academics from local institutions.

According to David Dill, professor of public policy analysis and education at the University of North Carolina, "Auditors review and verify the effectiveness of an institution's basic processes of academic quality assurance and improvement, including: (1) how an institution designs, monitors, and evaluates academic programs and degrees; (2) how an institution assesses, evaluates, and improves teaching and student learning; and (3) how an institution takes account of the views of external stakeholders in improving teaching and student learning" (http://www.unc.edu/courses/acaudit/whatisacademicaudit.html).

The process is structured somewhat like an accreditation process. It begins with the inspection of documents that describe the way the institution assesses its own performance. As a next step, a team of auditors visits the institution. Finally, the team writes a report that is made widely available. Because audit reports are made public, they are viewed as an important tool to ensure accountability. Public release also motivates institutions to take the process seriously.

Because the academic audit allows institutions to define their own quality assurance processes, it is more sensitive to the different roles, missions, and characteristics of institutions than are certain other approaches. As a result, it is particularly useful for systems with a diverse set of providers. Although it has been criticized for lack of attention to inputs and outcomes, it does not so much ignore outcomes as delegate responsibility for assessing outcomes to the provider.

The unit of analysis for academic audits is usually whole institutions, but the assessment could work with individual programs or departments. Each institution is assessed on its own terms, and reports are written with the institution in mind. Auditors deliberately avoid drawing comparisons among institutions. Current use of the academic audit is largely confined to higher education, although the principles could relate to training and professional development as well. In fact, the Teacher Education Accreditation Council incorporates the use of the academic audit in the accreditation of teaching programs.

## Model Two: Intermediary Conducts the Assessment

In Model Two, an intermediary conducts the actual assessment, including defining goals, measuring outcomes, and evaluating performance. Such an approach allows the intermediary to function as an independent check on quality. Except for corporate learning centers, most intermediaries are completely independent of the provider so that they can act as objective judges of quality. In this way, the model is well suited for the accountability function.

The independence of intermediaries also enables them to focus on system-level goals. State higher education coordinating and governing boards, for example, can manage the assessment process and choose performance measures that reflect state or system-level goals that individual institutions might not attend to. These issues, such as access and equity, are bigger than any individual institution and cut across schools. In this way, accountability systems provide states with leverage to influence institutions to focus on issues that they might otherwise overlook. In addition, some providers like having requirements imposed by external assessors, because it allows them an opportunity to motivate their employees to undertake changes they might otherwise resist.

The independence of the intermediary, however, can also undermine the value of the assessment. Any approach imposed from an external organization runs the risk of focusing on inappropriate measures and failing to reflect institutional goals. Moreover, although intermediaries might be better positioned than providers to reflect the goals of multiple stakeholder groups, it is unlikely that any one organization will be able to fairly and accurately reflect the goals of all relevant stakeholders. Indeed, intermediary assessment organizations often come under political pressure from one or more stakeholder groups. This pressure is perhaps one reason for the proliferation of such assessment organizations. Stakeholder groups that believe their needs are not reflected in existing assessment structures can create a new entity to ensure that their needs are represented. (Further examination of the constellation of assessment organizations, their goals and objectives, and the political forces impinging on them is needed.)

Model Two can be considered the most traditional model used by intermediaries. Organizations that use a Model Two assessment approach include state higher education governing and coordinating boards, *U.S. News & World Report,* and accreditation agencies that use the traditional approach to accreditation. The Malcolm Baldrige National Quality Award program also fits into this mold. Each of them is described briefly below.

### *State Higher Education Governing and Coordinating Boards*

State higher education boards work under the authority of the governor and legislature to ensure that postsecondary institutions operate collectively in ways that are aligned with state priorities and serve the public interest (McGuinness, 1997). Such quality assurance is accomplished through a third-party assessment of institutional performance relative to criteria established by the higher education board or its designee. State boards include governing boards and coordinating boards, which differ in their responsibilities, influence, and level of authority.

Most boards have created "accountability systems" to measure and ensure the quality of the institutions within their purview. Among the accountability systems in vogue today are performance indicators, report cards, and performance funding. Although accountability is the primary purpose of these systems, most states encourage institutions to use the data for self-improvement as well. Report cards, however, tend to be problematic in that they can enforce the lowest common denominator rather than high quality or even quality improvement. Because the "cut scores" for passing or failing on report card types of assessments are typically set arbitrarily, it is likely that most institutions will "pass," thus eliminating incentives for improvement. Even those institutions that do not pass may set their improvement goals only on whatever the pass score is, regardless of the quality or level of improvement that meeting those scores entails.

Accountability systems differ in their level of collaboration among stakeholders, providers, and intermediaries. Some higher education boards are more directive than others. When governing boards determine assessment goals, measures, and evaluations without substantial input from providers, conflict and resentment often follow. Institutional leaders may feel that the state is imposing standards on them that do not reflect the institution's actual quality. Other state boards are more collaborative and ask institutions to play a substantial role in establishing assessment goals and methods. Although this approach leads to more acceptance of assessment by providers, it is time-consuming and costly.

The information gathered through these accountability systems is used in at least four ways:

- *Funding.* Some states link a percentage of funding to institutional performance. Tennessee awards 2 to 5 percent of its instructional budget based on assessment results. In theory, South Carolina awards 100 percent of funding based on performance, but in practice a much smaller percentage (approximately 5 percent) depends on assessment results (Schmidt, 1999).
- *Program Planning and Elimination.* Assessment results may contribute to decision making about academic programs. For example, based on its review of assessment data, the Illinois Board of Higher Education in 1992 recommended the elimination, consolidation, or reduction of 190 programs at public universities, including 7 percent of all undergraduate programs, among other changes.
- *Improvement.* In many states, individual campuses are encouraged to use assessment results for self-improvement purposes. The degree to which this actually occurs is unknown.
- *Public Information.* Assessment results also provide a means of informing the public about their state's higher education system. Thus, some states publish report cards for either the system as a whole or for individual institutions.

The effectiveness of state accountability systems is uneven. At best, the efforts may lead to quality improvements and better alignment between higher education and state policy goals. At worst, the efforts create dissension, force institutions to redirect resources away from other, arguably more valuable activities, and provide little insight into the performance of higher education institutions and systems.

## U.S. News & World Report

*U.S. News & World Report* has devised criteria for evaluating colleges and universities and uses those criteria to rank institutions yearly. The company plays the role of an intermediary and sees itself as one potential source of information to customers of higher education. The process does not encourage any formal collaboration among the stakeholders, providers, and the intermediary. *U.S. News & World Report* determines the assessment criteria, conducts the analysis, and provides the results to consumers. The rankings are based on quality measures determined by the publication, including, for example, reputation of the school, selectivity, faculty resources, and financial resources. The ranking formula weights the indicators by level of importance, imposing a model of what a "good college" or "good graduate program" is. In doing so, the *U.S. News & World Report* rankings system implicitly attributes goals to institutions and their stakeholders.

## Accrediting Agencies

Accreditation is another example of intermediary assessment of provider organizations. Accreditation in U.S. higher education determines whether an institution or a program meets threshold quality criteria (traditionally determined by the accrediting body) and therefore certifies to the public the existence of minimum educational standards. It is voluntary and is mostly carried out by eight regional commissions.[6] These commissions are responsible for accrediting whole institutions. In addition, there are dozens of national associations that offer recognized specialized and professional accreditation for programs or other academic units in an institution, or for freestanding single-purpose institutions.

Accreditation has primarily been about accountability, but efforts are under way to make the process more flexible so that institutions can use the process for self-improvement. Some accreditation commissions are working more collaboratively than others with providers.

Accreditation is a multistep process. The program or institution first conducts a self-study, using guidelines from the accrediting agency. Following the self-study, the accrediting team visits the institution, where the team meets with a range of institutional representatives. Based on the visit and the materials provided by the institution, the review team evaluates such measures as educational objectives, programs and curricula, degree programs, faculty, student services, student progress, admission policies and practices, student recruitment, and management. It submits a report to the accrediting agency, which provides a formal report to the program or institution. After the institution is given an opportunity to respond, the accrediting agency decides whether to grant accreditation. Although the result is made public, only the program and institution are provided the details that support the decision.

The accreditation process can be extremely expensive, particularly for major universities that go through the process multiple times for various specializations or programs as well as institutional or regional accreditation. Accreditation tends to occur on a ten-year cycle, however, so institutions do not have to go through the process very often (the exception again being research universities with multiple departments undergoing specialized accreditation).

### *Malcolm Baldrige National Quality Award*

The Malcolm Baldrige National Quality Award program is another example of Model Two, but it differs from other Model Two approaches in that providers must actively choose to participate in the program. The program seeks to assess the overall performance management system of participating organizations and to recognize those that excel. The objective of the award is to help U.S. organizations meet the highest standards by improving current practices in performance and quality.

The Baldrige Award program was established in the late 1980s as many industry and government leaders recognized the need to establish a standard of excellence for organizations striving for quality and efficiency. These efforts resulted in the passage of the Malcolm Baldrige National Quality Act of 1987 (Public Law 100–107). Over the years, the award has gained significant prestige in industry and government. Because of high demand for the program, in 1999 it was expanded to include organizations from education and health care sectors as well.

The Department of Commerce is responsible for the award, and the National Institute of Standards and Technology (NIST) manages the program with assistance from the American Society for Quality. A board of overseers, made up of members from industry handpicked by the Secretary of Commerce, directs the award program and determines whether the evaluation process and requirements are adequate.

The annual award is presented to three organizations from five different sectors, which include manufacturing, service, small business, healthcare, and education. The board of examiners, comprising expert volunteers and representing the range of sectors, conducts evaluations of all participating organizations and recommends approval of award winners to NIST. Regardless of award status, each organization is given detailed feedback of strengths and areas for improvement. Award recipients are required to share their performance and quality strategies with other institutions that may be interested in improving their own standards.

The purpose of the award is to help organizations improve and gain a competitive edge by delivering better value to customers and by improving their performance. The award has three main objectives:

- To promote awareness of the importance of quality improvement to the national economy
- To recognize organizations that have improved substantially in products, services, and overall competitive performance
- To foster sharing of information about best practices among U.S. organizations (National Institute of Standards and Technology, 1995).

This purpose is linked to the Department of Commerce's mission of improving the competitiveness of each participating organization in the global marketplace.

The award criteria set standards for the level of assessment that institutions must undertake and evaluate them along specified dimensions related to quality. Organizations volunteer to participate in the program's assessment process because they view it as a means of self-improvement. Many organizations report having better employee relations and higher productivity and profitability as a result of their participation. Companies also report improved customer satisfaction after implementing Baldrige recommendations.

Organizations from several sectors, including manufacturing, service, and small business, participate in this program. The Baldrige model assumes that different business sectors share common core requirements for excellence in quality and productivity. It is the manner in which these requirements are addressed that may vary among organizations. Because the measures are not specific, the approach is adaptable; the focus of assessment is on outcomes and common requirements rather than on detailed procedures.

Among the business community, the award is held in high esteem. Winning companies become quality advocates for other institutions and inform them on the benefits of using the Baldrige framework. In fact, companies are also asked to provide information on their performance strategies and methods so that others may learn from them.

### The Problem of Compliance

Intermediary assessors using a Model Two approach are often caught off guard by institutional resistance (National Center for Higher Education Management Systems, 1996). For example, in state higher education systems, some state boards have proposed to assess graduation rates, while community college representatives argue that only one-third of their students aspire to graduate. In New Mexico, a report card requirement was dropped because of criticism from institutions that the diversity of institutions, missions, and students made institutional comparisons unreliable or only minimally indicative of institutional performance (J. Cole, Nettles, and Sharp, 1997). Negotiating such issues and reaching a compromise that satisfies both the assessor and the assessed can take tremendous time and effort.

Even when assessors can agree on measures and overcome resistance, they are not necessarily certain that accountability-based initiatives will lead to institutional improvements (Boyer, Ewell, Finney, and Mingle, 1987). Many suspect that accountability endeavors produce a compliance response that is divorced from improvement (Aper, Cuver, and Hinkle, 1990; Ewell, 1993; El-Khawas, 1995; Steele and Lutz, 1995). In the higher education sector, state initiatives that prescribe standardized measures may be less well accepted internally and thus less useful for informing institutional improvement than those that permit institutions to use locally developed assessment instruments (Ewell, 1987a; Jacobi, Astin, and Ayala, 1987; Ory, 1991; Terenzini, 1989).

Institutional improvement is unlikely to result from an assessment process that is fundamentally flawed, even if the assessor does gain compliance. The *U.S. News & World Report* rankings have drawn criticism for the way that measures are weighted in an approach that "lacks any defensible empirical or theoretical basis" (Reisberg, 2000, p. 1). *U.S. News* has also been criticized for changing the weighting method periodically, preventing accurate comparisons from year to year and impeding the use of this assessment system to track improvement.

Organizational theory posits that five strategies exist for responding to external requests or constraints: complying, compromising, avoiding, defying, and manipulating (Oliver, 1991). Although complying may be the most ideal response, from the point of view of the organization asking for compliance, it is difficult to achieve. Even when institutions intend to comply, they may lack the know-how to do so effectively. In addition, avoidance can be masked by faked compliance. The organization may appear to comply with the request but not actually follow through. In certain situations, the organization may defy the external request, such as when the perceived costs of resistance are low, when internal values diverge from external mandates, or when organizations believe they can demonstrate the rationality of their alternative conduct (Oliver, 1991). Finally, manipulation is an option, with organizations attempting to co-opt, influence, or control mandates. Manipulation is often seen in cases where the external assessor's office is staffed by people who have close relationships with those they are attempting to assess.

Organizations are most likely to comply in several circumstances: when they are highly dependent on the institution exerting the pressure,[7] when there is a legal or regulatory apparatus to enforce compliance, when the expectations are already very broadly diffused or supported or when the mandates do not impinge on the autonomy of core areas, and when the organization believes that complying will benefit it through conferring a positive reward such as resources or prestige or reducing negative sanctions such as censorious judgments (Oliver, 1991).

Many examples exist of assessors who do not have direct authority over the assessed yet still achieve compliance. For example, to compete for the Baldrige Award (which is a voluntary choice), institutions acquiesce to the call for information because they can gain prestige from compliance. In this case, the institutions believe that they will benefit from complying (and they know that they will not be punished). Nursing and some subdisciplines of business, law, medical, and other professional schools comply with external assessments in the form of licensing and certifying examinations. Students must pass these exams to be able to work in their chosen field. These providers comply with the assessment of their students to gain legitimacy. Students would not attend these institutions if they could not be certified to work in their field. Other organizations provide incentives to achieve compliance. The Kentucky Council on Postsecondary Education, for example, uses incentive funding to persuade higher education institutions to develop programs or services in line with its vision for higher education in the state.

Authority relationships influence not only compliance but also what is done with the resulting assessment information. If there is no structure in place to sanction an institution that does not perform well or to demand that an institution improve, there is little likelihood that the assessment will have any impact. Of course, this is an issue regardless of the assessment model chosen, but studies have shown that assessments that allow the provider more control over the process, as in Models One and Three, are more likely to lead to improvements (Aper and Hinkle, 1991; Ewell, 1991).

## Model Three: Provider Conducts the Assessment

In our third model, providers conduct their own self-assessment to ensure quality and productivity without the involvement of any intermediary. Its purpose is improvement—a means of assuring customers they are getting what they need—rather than accountability. Some of the most innovative approaches to provider assessment, however, build in greater versatility: they are multipurpose assessments designed to incorporate the perspectives of a range of stakeholders. The best examples of this model are higher education institutions or programs, both nonprofit and for-profit.

## *The University of Phoenix*

The University of Phoenix, formed in 1976, is a for-profit higher education institution. Offering mainly night classes, it serves working adults, generally thirty-five to thirty-nine years old. Students take five- or six-week-long courses, one at a time. Many of the faculty are part-time instructors who have full-time jobs elsewhere. The school serves approximately 49,000 students at 65 campuses in 15 states, Puerto Rico, Vancouver, British Columbia, and via distance education. About 9,500 students are served via the distance education program.

The University of Phoenix has a centrally developed curriculum for every program, which facilitates centralized assessment. No matter who is teaching a course, certain baseline content is observed, and specific outcomes are expected (so students know what is expected of them). All the courses are developed by content experts. The general education curriculum consists of courses that focus on written communication skills, oral presentation skills, critical-thinking skills, problem-solving skills, self-reflection, and an appreciation of diversity. In addition, the university offers certificate and degree programs in a number of fields, such as business, health care, education, counseling and human services, technology, and management. Campuses cannot develop new credit-bearing courses.

Assessment practices were not developed until the mid-1980s. The University of Phoenix has a number of different mechanisms in place for measuring quality, most of which were originally implemented to demonstrate the school's quality to the external world but are now used for internal improvement purposes as well. For example, faculty can be recruited and trained.

The purpose of the assessment process is to measure value added and customer satisfaction, and to ensure that certain inputs and processes are in place across the campuses. The portfolio of assessment practices enables the

University of Phoenix to measure the quality of the curriculum as well as the quality of administrative practices.

The university has regional accreditation from the Commission on Institutions of Higher Education of the North Central Association of Colleges and Schools. It also has programmatic accreditation in nursing and counseling. The North Central regional accrediting agency is moving toward outcomes assessment, which suits the university's purposes well.

The University of Phoenix has a number of mechanisms in place for measuring quality, most of which were originally intended to demonstrate their quality to potential customers—both employers and learners—but are now used for program improvement as well. The primary assessment tools are the following:

- *Student testing.* All students are tested at the beginning and end of each course to measure what they have learned. The institution also uses test results for self-improvement. If students do poorly on a certain section of the test at one campus, administrators work with that campus to improve instruction of the material. If students everywhere do poorly on a section, the university revises the course curriculum.
- *Surveys of customer and employer satisfaction.* Students are surveyed for their evaluation of the quality of teaching, curriculum, books, and supplemental materials. Alumni and employers are also regularly surveyed to determine whether University of Phoenix graduates have the right skills and are getting promoted. Beyond such surveys, students also participate in exit interviews to gauge their satisfaction. Results of such activities, along with information on other issues such as class size, are provided in quarterly (and sometimes monthly) reports that are sent to stakeholders. Campuses also use these reports for program improvement.
- *Reports on the quality and efficiency of business operations.* These reports compare the campuses in terms of their services and business operations. They assess such things as student numbers and whether learning centers are turning their paperwork in on time.

Like the corporate model of continuous process improvement, the university's ongoing evaluation of the data collected by these means encourages individual campuses to improve student learning. Although campuses are not penalized for poor performance, they are compared with one another. The university's philosophy is managing by exception: it looks at outliers and then works with them to improve. It has also set up a buddy/mentorship program so schools that are not performing well in a particular area are matched with a campus that is doing well in that area.

## *The Urban Universities Portfolio Project*

A group of urban public universities have come up with an innovative new method for communicating their difference from traditional public universities and assessing the quality and effectiveness of their institutions. Six universities—Indiana University Purdue University Indianapolis, University of Illinois at Chicago, Portland State University, California State University at Sacramento, University of Massachusetts at Boston, and Georgia State University—participate in the Urban Universities Portfolio Project funded by The Pew Charitable Trusts (Cambridge and others, 2001). All of these institutions serve primarily nontraditional students, many of whom are older than most college students and working full time, and many of whom are first-generation college students from diverse racial and ethnic backgrounds. Most of them attend classes on evenings and weekends or enroll in distance education courses. Aware of their special mandate, these universities collaborated to design an assessment method that would hold them accountable for making progress toward the goals they set themselves and provide them a tool for improving their educational practices. Although each university is developing its own portfolio that will eventually be published on the Web, all six of them will combine their efforts to define common objectives and outcome measures that reflect their similar missions. This process will help establish that urban public universities should not be judged by the same standards used for traditional universities. A common assessment approach will also allow students and policymakers to draw meaningful comparisons among urban public universities.

An additional objective of the project is to improve the understanding of the distinguishing features of urban public universities among both internal and external stakeholders. The project calls for close collaboration with representative stakeholders. Two groups of external constituents have been established. Both the National Advisory Board and the Institutional Review Board comprise distinguished leaders from business, government, and education. The role of the National Advisory Board is to advise the project about its aims, practices, and progress by reviewing the evolving set of core goals, indicators, and measures and by keeping current on issues facing urban public schools. Board members include key university officials and figures from higher education and accrediting organizations. The Institutional Review Board works closely with the participating urban universities, advising on portfolio development. Members include college deans, directors of accrediting associations, professors, and provosts from a range of institutions. Although these boards include external members, we consider the project an example of Model Three, because it was motivated by and is primarily run by the providers. It is likely that several accrediting agencies that are closely involved in the project will adopt some of the project's practices, which would be an example of Model Two.

In the strictest interpretation of Model Three, there is no role for an intermediary. We did observe cases, however, in which an intermediary with no formal authority to assess providers offers recommendations for improving the assessment process and suggests assessment tools, methods, and rationales on which providers and stakeholders can draw. In these circumstances, the intermediary can help promote quality by offering different types of assistance, although it does not actually ensure quality.

The U.S. Department of Transportation is an example in which an intermediary organization can guide the self-assessment efforts of individual providers. The DOT Learning and Development Program has developed a policy guide called the "Learning and Development Framework," which is designed for use by managers and supervisors in implementing DOT's education and development policies and programs. The published framework provides recommendations for assessment of program activities as well, although the assessment is carried out at the operating administration level. In other words, the operating administrations determine for themselves whether their education and professional development activities are meeting the goals as defined by the Learning and Development Program.

Corporate learning organizations also often play such a role in Model Three. Many serve as advisers to the business units that actually provide the training. They can be information clearinghouses, offering assistance on everything from curriculum development to assessment.

## Model Four: Student Competencies Are Assessed

Model Four represents a completely different approach to assessment, one that focuses attention on the student rather than the provider. The previous approaches, which focus on the provider, implicitly assume that if the institution is good, students who pass through the institution will learn what they need to learn. In addition, specific information on student performance is an element in most assessments; evidence of students' performance, improvement, or achievement (e.g., pass rates on licensure exams) is considered a measure of an institution's success or failure. What makes Model Four different is that the assessment essentially ignores the provider (for more information on this trend, see Adelman, 2000). In some cases, individuals need not attend an institution or take a course to achieve certification. Instead, they may learn skills or concepts on the job or through a CD-ROM, or they may be self-taught. The end result of the assessment accomplished through Model Four is the certification of student competencies. Therefore, the Model Four approach is often called *competency-based assessment.*

In recent years, business leaders and educators have focused increased attention on the concept of student competencies as an innovative approach to education and training, and assessment. The competency-based approach allows educators to organize courses and instruction around the gap between what students already know and what they should know to demonstrate a level of proficiency in a particular area.

In recent years, business leaders and educators have focused increased attention on the concept of student competencies as an innovative approach to education and training, and assessment.

Competencies can be defined in several ways. As discussed in the previous section, defining competencies can be a part of Phase One assessment for a system, as in the Air Force example. The most common method is to identify tasks that define competency in a certain domain and assess whether tasks are completed to conclude that proficiency has been achieved. Critics argue that this process oversimplifies performance in the real world by ignoring the relationship between tasks and other factors that influence performance. Another approach looks only at general characteristics needed for effective job performance, such as critical-thinking skills or communication skills. This method ignores the need for different skills in different domains and the need to transfer expertise from one area to another. A more integrated approach combines defined tasks as well as crosscutting skills to identify the knowledge, skills, and abilities needed to perform effectively in particular domain areas. In this approach, "competence is conceived of as complex structuring of attributes needed for intelligent performance in specific situations" (Gonczi, 1994, p. 29). Competency-based education and training is being used in government, private industry, and higher education as a way to meet the wide-ranging needs of a diverse group of learners. The following examples highlight Microsoft's technical certification programs, the Department of Labor's SCANS Initiative, and Western Governors University, a leader in the competency-based approach to higher education.

### Microsoft's Technical Certification Programs

Microsoft has developed a well known and widely recognized set of technical certification programs. "Certification provides professionals with a valuable credential that recognizes their skills with the most advanced Microsoft technology. Certification also provides businesses with an objective way to identify individuals who can help them compete more successfully in their industry using Microsoft technology" (http://www.microsoft.com/trainingandservices/default.asp?PageID=mcp&PageCall=certifications&SubSite=cert).

Individuals can achieve technical certifications in one of several areas by taking a series of examinations. The Microsoft Web site provides information on the exams required for each certification, skills being measured in a particular exam, ways to prepare for the exam (including official courses offered by Microsoft, books, CD-ROMs, on-line content, and videos), and practice exams that measure technical proficiency and expertise in specific areas. "As an industry leader in professional certification, Microsoft is at the forefront of testing methodology. Our exams and corresponding certifications are developed to validate mastery of critical competencies. Exams are developed with the input of professionals in the industry and reflect how Microsoft products are used in organizations throughout the world" (www.microsoft.com). The examinations are offered by two independent companies at testing sites worldwide.

### The Department of Labor's SCANS Initiative

The federal government has also recognized the benefits of conducting job analysis to identify the necessary competencies for certain jobs. The Secretary of Labor's Commission on Achieving Necessary Skills (SCANS) was undertaken with the intent of linking competencies and skills needed by the business community and government to what is taught in schools. SCANS aims to "define the skills needed for employment, propose acceptable levels of proficiency, suggest effective ways to assess proficiency and develop a dissemination strategy" (U.S. Department of Labor, 1991, p. xv). Although SCANS acknowledges that technical expertise varies among industries, it posits that the basic competencies, or "workplace know-how," are the same for all types of jobs. They identified five major categories of skills needed in all industries: resources, interpersonal, information, systems, and technology. In addition, according to SCANS, students need a three-part foundation consisting of basic skills, thinking skills, and personal qualities.

### Western Governors University

The Western Governors University (WGU), established in 1997, has been a leader in higher education's competency-based approach to education. The university was created to address several challenges, including "a wide geographic dispersion of students; nontraditional students, such as adults employed full time, seeking part-time enrollment; scarcity of workers in certain highly trained occupations; rising student costs of attaining higher education; existing and potential duplication of effort among states in developing courses and programs; failure of existing higher educational institutions to recognize and acknowledge skills and abilities [that] students already possess; and inadequate information to students about educational opportunities and choices" (Testa, 1999, p. 3).

WGU differs from traditional institutions of higher education in that the degree and certificate programs are defined by a set of competencies that students must demonstrate rather than a set of courses they must take. Thus, WGU's primary effort is directed toward defining an appropriate set of competencies, developing valid and reliable methods for measuring those competencies, and helping students identify learning opportunities that can help them acquire competencies they are lacking. The attainment of a degree or certificate is based not on credit hours but on the successful completion of a set of competency tests. In fact, students may earn a degree or certification without taking courses if they can demonstrate competency in a domain area (Testa, 1999).

WGU faculty members play a key role in the design and development of programs and assessment instruments. Actual courses are delivered by distance learning providers, which are approved by WGU for providing education that fosters the development of specific competencies.

Competency-based education benefits students because it gives them recognition of past achievements, portability of course credits, and a system for lifelong learning (Paulson and Ewell, 1999). Institutions value competency-based education and training because they encourage stakeholders to closely examine what is important for students to know and instructors to teach as well as help in targeting scarce resources where they will be most effective (Mager, 1997).

## Strengths and Weaknesses of the Four Approaches

Table 1 summarizes the strengths and weaknesses of all four models. One of the primary strengths of Model One is the flexibility achieved by its focus on process. Because the providers are allowed to conduct their own assessment, they can establish the goals and measures that best reflect their institutions. The review then focuses on whether the goals are reasonable and whether the measures are valid and reliable indicators of achievement of those goals. This

**TABLE 1**
**Strengths and Weaknesses of the Four Assessment Models**

| Model | Strengths | Weaknesses |
|---|---|---|
| One: Provider conducts assessment, intermediary reviews provider's assessment process | Flexibility of approach can accommodate diverse institutions; approach promotes program improvement | Less suitable for purpose of accountability; can promote quality but not ensure it |
| Two: Intermediary designs assessment process and conducts assessment | Independent check on quality; well suited for accountability; can focus on system-level goals | Approach may be overly standardized and thus neglect differences among institutions; may be driven by goals that have little relation to the quality of education; may lead to institutional resistance; may have little effect on quality improvement |
| Three: Provider designs assessment process and conducts assessment | Flexibility accommodates differences among institutions; stimulus to self-improvement | Less suitable for accountability; not useful for assessing system-level needs |
| Four: Provider or intermediary assesses student competencies | Focuses on measuring student learning; relates student learning to workplace competencies | Time-consuming and expensive; difficult to measure less defined and more abstract competencies; may be more suitable for professional education and training than for traditional academic institutions |

flexibility makes the model ideal for a heterogeneous system, where it can be difficult to define meaningful measures of quality that are appropriate for all institutions.

Although Model One is ideally suited for program improvement, it is less suited for accountability. One of the major drawbacks of this approach is that the intermediary does not assess actual educational or training outcomes. The assumption, however, is that good internal processes for assessment will automatically lead to improved outcomes. Providers may choose to examine outcomes as part of their process.

Model Two, on the other hand, has the advantage of providing an independent perspective on quality and productivity. Because an intermediary conducts the assessment, the approach is well suited for accountability and can embrace systemwide issues, such as access and equity. The main disadvantage of this approach is that it fails to allow for important distinctions in mission and emphasis among provider institutions. It also imposes burdensome data collection requirements on institutions that are not always used for the purposes of self-improvement. In fact, little evidence exists that state accountability systems have led to improvements in students' learning; this approach is the one most likely to meet resistance from provider institutions.

Another potential challenge facing Model Two is that intermediaries may pick inappropriate goals and thus provide information that is misleading or irrelevant to customers and providers. For example, despite its popularity, *U.S. News & World Report* has been condemned for placing too much emphasis on reputation, for ignoring student learning, for stifling diversity by using the same yardstick for all institutions, and for frequently changing the ranking methodology. Even corporate learning organizations, the most "inside" of the intermediaries, are sometimes criticized by staff for being out of touch with the profit-making mission of the company. Accrediting agencies have come under attack for having a standard set of criteria that do not reflect the diversity of institutional missions and for focusing too heavily on inputs and not on educational outcomes.

In contrast to Model Two, the primary strength of Model Three is the flexibility it leaves providers to define their own goals, assess their performance based on those goals, and learn from the process how they can best improve. The lack of external oversight or review of the provider's process, however, implies that Model Three cannot easily be used for accountability purposes. In addition, Model Three provides no mechanism for assessing system-level needs.

Model Four is appealing because it "enables us to come closer than we have in the past to assessing what we want to assess—the capacity of the professional to integrate knowledge, values, attitudes and skills in the world of practice" (Gonczi, 1994, p. 28). But it is time-consuming and expensive to define relevant competencies, develop ways to measure them, and update the definitions and measures. Moreover, some competencies are easier to define than others. Although it may be relatively easy to specify the competencies that a computer systems administrator must have, it is more difficult to specify the competencies that a plant manager needs to have. Many observers believe it is doubtful that a competency-based education approach will be embraced by the academic community (Carnevale, 2000).

This section has provided an overview of the approaches used by various organizations engaged in the assessment of education and professional development activities. We were not able to identify a single best model; each model has its own strengths and weaknesses. The next section discusses some of the issues an assessor should consider in selecting among the different models.

# Choosing the Right Model
# for Phase Two

THIS SECTION DISCUSSES how to determine which model to select as an assessment approach in cases where one is free to choose an approach that is best suited to a certain education environment. New assessment processes should be created with care so that they fit logically into the network of assessors and reporting requirements that already exists. A single institution is often beholden to several assessment processes. A state university, for example, must be accredited as an institution, must have its preprofessional programs accredited separately, must be certified to receive Title IV funding, must be authorized by the state to offer degrees, and is probably subject to assessment by a state higher education governing board for accountability purposes. Multiple assessments are costly and time-consuming and often impose duplication of effort on institutions providing data to separate assessors.

Our analysis suggests that selecting an assessment approach should begin with a consideration of the purpose of the assessment and be founded on a clear understanding of the education system's characteristics, including the nature of the assessor's position within that system.

## Purposes of Assessment

Any new assessor's office needs to first identify the problem it has been established to address and then articulate its mission in terms of that problem. "Considerable experience teaches us that we must be very clear about the nature of the particular problem we are trying to address through measurement, lest the measurement itself become the end of policy" (Ewell, 1999a, p. 155). New assessment systems are usually established to address a problem that is not being monitored by existing assessors or that could be better addressed by an alternative approach or an agency with a distinctive competency. A newly established assessor needs to focus on this problem and develop a strategic vision for addressing it and a plan for implementing that vision (Levy and others, 2001). This process should help clarify whether the purpose of the assessment is primarily accountability or primarily improvement.

There are at least three contexts in which state higher education coordinating boards, a type of intermediary that is often interested in both improvement and accountability, typically favor accountability-based assessment over improvement-oriented assessment:

- *When a system that is moving from a centralized to a decentralized process for managing providers.* States that relinquish control of program planning and curriculum design for their higher education institutions do so with the expectation that these institutions will demonstrate that they are maintaining quality.
- *When resource allocations must be monitored.* States become more concerned with accountability as they provide increased funding to higher education institutions. They want to ensure that recipient institutions use these resources, which are scarce, effectively and efficiently (Stevens and Hamlett, 1983). Legislatures and the public in general often call for greater accountability without regard for improvement (Steele and Lutz, 1995).
- *When there is a call for change.* This type of assessment can be used to hold institutions accountable to meeting specific goals and therefore change behavior more quickly. External constituents used this type of assessment in the 1980s to monitor reforms in state higher education systems (see, e.g., Association of American Colleges, 1985; National Institute of Education, 1984; Bennett, 1984).

Assessment for improvement purposes, on the other hand, is typically undertaken when quality improvement is the desired result and when there is no need for comparative data among different institutions. For example, several countries in Europe and Asia have instituted academic audits as their assessment process for their higher education institutions. Academic audits allow educational providers to conduct their own internal assessment, while an intermediary evaluates the process of this self-assessment. These countries are not interested in comparing their higher education institutions with each other, but they do want to ensure that they are constantly focusing on internal improvement.

As described earlier, the assessment process used for accountability differs from approaches devoted to quality improvement. In assessing for accountability, an external body controls the assessment, setting the goals against which performance will be assessed. A state board, for example, might hold an institution accountable for contributing to the state's economic development. This goal may not have been a goal of the provider's, but because the assessment is for accountability purposes, an intermediary determines the goals. In assessment for accountability, an external evaluator also typically delineates the measures and evaluates the results. These results are used to judge the provider's performance, often providing a reward or a sanction based on performance. This is the approach taken in Model Two.

In assessment for improvement purposes, the process is structured so that the provider can use the resulting information to make improvements. Typically, a provider, such as a college or a department within a university, delineates its own goals for improvement and conducts an assessment to determine how well it is meeting those goals. The measures used in such an assessment typically reflect input, process, output, and outcome variables, so that the assessor can understand what inputs and processes lead to what outcomes. Understanding these relationships allows a provider to identify the changes (to inputs, processes, or outputs) required to generate improved performance in the organization. Models One and Three are most suitable for this purpose. Model Four may also contribute indirectly to the provider's improvement. In fact, an assessor need not commit to a single model for quality improvement assessments but choose different models for different assessment tasks in the system.

Is it possible to design an approach that provides both accountability and program improvement? Many commentators hold that the two objectives are simply incompatible, arguing that what intermediaries typically need to hold providers accountable to (uniform information that is easily communicable to external audiences) is not what the institutions being assessed need (information that links assessment results to specific institutional experiences) (J. Cole, Nettles, and Sharp, 1997). Moreover, assessment data are gathered and reported much differently if the purpose is to reward and sanction rather than to identify opportunities for improvement. Institutions have incentives to package their data as positively as possible—even to provide misleading data— if they know they will be compared with others and that their results will be used in making summative decisions on funding or continued existence.

Other commentators believe that assessment for improvement and assessment for accountability need not be mutually exclusive (Palomba and Banta, 1999). Half the existing state boards maintain that they have policies designed to both ensure quality and hold institutions accountable (J. Cole, Nettles, and Sharp, 1997). Palomba and Banta (1999) argue that it is possible, albeit challenging, to develop measurements that are meaningful both locally and to higher-ups. Ewell (1987b, 1990) approves of state initiatives that require institutions to report on improvements made based on information gathered for accountability assessments because they should promote greater institutional support for those assessments and lead to quality improvements.

Model One is the most promising approach for combining the two purposes. It has the potential to hold the provider accountable to at least a standard baseline of quality audit while assuring sound institutional processes for quality improvement. In addition, the intermediary can go beyond solely monitoring the process. Model One can be modified to include features that provide for accountability, such as minimum standards (Massy and French, 1999). It can require that the process contain a specific task, such as evaluating teacher quality, or it can set limits on the goals the institutions can have. For example, program faculty in institutions that are members of the Teacher Education Accreditation Council are required to accept the goal of preparing "competent, caring, and qualified teachers." Intermediaries could also require the provider to communicate the results of the assessments, even though these results would not be comparable with other institutional results (given the autonomy of each provider in establishing its own process). Finally, the intermediary can ask the provider to describe how the results of the process are used to make improvements, which could contribute toward both accountability and improvement.

Although Model Four focuses on students' competencies, it indirectly holds institutions accountable by withholding competency status from students that have not received the requisite education from specific providers. These providers must change to maintain their ability to attract students; in this way, the assessment process stimulates improvement while indirectly holding providers accountable for change.

## Level of Authority

Another key factor in considering an assessment model is the degree of authority the assessor has over provider institutions. Is there a formal reporting arrangement between the assessor and the providers? Does the assessor have the ability to offer incentives or impose sanctions to achieve compliance?

If the assessor has formal authority over providers and the power to offer rewards or impose sanctions for nonobservance, then any of the approaches to assessment could be successfully implemented. If, on the other hand, the assessor has limited authority over providers, the choices narrow. Because Models One and Three provide more control to the providers, they are more likely to achieve their objectives without strong external incentives. Model Four focuses on student competencies, so the issue of authority over providers is not relevant. Model Two, on the other hand, frequently elicits institutional resistance because it is imposed from the outside. Without a strong position of authority over providers in the system, that approach is less likely to succeed. Even in cases where compliance may appear to be forthcoming, the data supplied by providers may not accurately reflect the provider. For example, representatives from *U.S. News & World Report* encounter low levels of resistance in gathering data, as most institutions do not want to be left out of the publication's ranking edition. The extent to which the *U.S. News & World Report* staff are collecting reliable data, accurately capturing the essence of quality, or spurring institutional improvement is unknown, however.

Authority relationships influence not only compliance but also impact. If no structure is in place to sanction an institution that does not perform well or demand that an institution improve, there is little likelihood that the assessment will have any effect. Although this is an issue regardless of the assessment model chosen, in Models One and Three, because the assessor allows the provider more control of the process, results of assessment tend to be used to make changes for improvement (Aper and Hinkle, 1991; Ewell, 1991).[8]

## Level of Resources

Available resources—including size of budget, staff, level of expertise, and credibility among key stakeholder groups—are another important consideration in choosing an assessment model. Assessment can be an extremely expensive endeavor in many regards. Extensive information makes up the base of any assessment task. Staff members are needed to gather information, forge relationships, and develop the assessment model. Expertise is needed to carry out an assessment. Depending on the existing level of expertise, the assessor may need to hire additional (permanent or temporary) staff or train existing ones. Conducting an assessment is labor-, time-, and energy-intensive. Credibility is another important resource for the assessor. Do key stakeholders believe that the assessor has the expertise required to design and implement the assessment, and do they value the assessor's judgment? Before choosing an assessment model, the assessor should consider whether the available resources are sufficient for the task.

Although it is obviously important to have enough resources to conduct high-quality assessment, it is difficult to say exactly how much is necessary. We were unable to find systematic information on the cost of implementing different types of assessment models, although we did get a general sense of the resources required through some of our case studies. Models Two and Four are the more resource-intensive models for an intermediary. In Model Two, the intermediary not only evaluates the results of assessment but also designs the assessment and typically the instruments that will be used to gather data as well. Although often ignored, substantial resources can also be required to overcome resistance to assessment on the part of providers. In Model Four, the intermediary tests student competencies, which also entails extensive resources for instrument design, data collection, and evaluation of the results. Moreover, the assessor's credibility determines whether the certification is of any value to students.

Although Model One may be less expensive, the intermediary still bears many costs. New staff may need to be hired, and existing staff will likely need training. Costs will also be incurred in establishing relationships with providers, developing guidelines for providers to use in monitoring quality, and gathering information. Although these costs for the intermediary should be less than those that would be expended under Model Two, the costs to the providers themselves may be more substantial under both Models One and Three. Because of the high cost to providers under these models, it may take more time and energy on the part of the intermediary to convince providers of the importance of conducting a Model One– or Model Three–type assessment. If Model Three is chosen, the costs to the intermediary are the lowest.

# Centralization of Operations

The degree to which a system is centralized should also affect the choice of an assessment model. Specifically, the way in which a system has structured its information, policies, administration, and curriculum processes affects the efficacy of assessment under different models. Some systems, such as corporate learning centers or for-profit universities, are highly centralized in everything from curriculum development to data collection. At the University of Phoenix, for example, a central office develops all the course curricula, specifies intended course outcomes, and gathers data on both providers and customers into a central database. Therefore, much of the work of assessment (identifying the educational goals) is completed early in the process in a consistent manner. The central office that constructs the goals is also responsible for measuring attainment of those goals.

Other systems, however, are decentralized in their curriculum and delivery process but centralized in their data collection. In Texas, the Higher Education Coordinating Board oversees a heterogeneous and decentralized system of institutions but has worked hard to ensure that they collect and manage extensive amounts of data. This board can track students across colleges or systems and into the workforce by linking Social Security numbers to Texas workforce commission data. As a result, institutions are aware of the paths taken by their graduates. Community colleges can track both transfer and graduation rates, and all institutions can see where (and whether) their graduates end up working (for those who stay in Texas). Having such centralized data can be instrumental to successful assessment.

In terms of the models, Model Two works well in a system in which the intermediary controls the educational components of developing the curriculum and designing the delivery. In such a centralized system, the coordinating office or intermediary not only is involved in setting the initial educational goals but also deals with providers that are dependent on the expertise and guidance of the centralized entity. Such providers would tend to trust the judgment of and relinquish assessment authority to the centralized entity. Model Two is also easier to implement if the intermediary has access to centralized databases. In systems without either centralized data or centralized curriculum processes, Models One and Three may be a better fit. Under Model Four, information about students, rather than providers, needs to be centralized to some extent so that the assessor has a way of conveying whether or not the student has achieved certification. The most complicated environments for assessment are those in which both educational services and information gathering are decentralized and no central office controls curriculum and delivery and has access to little centralized data.

# System Heterogeneity

In the choice of an assessment model, it is important to consider the heterogeneity of educational providers in the system. Important dimensions of heterogeneity include size, geographic location, relationships to stakeholders, and organizational affiliation of providers. (Organizational affiliation can include whether the providers are part of the system being considered or external to it.) Heterogeneity of mission is especially important. Within an educational system, providers may offer a wide variety of educational opportunities, ranging from an hour-long course to a doctoral degree program. The greater this variance, the more difficult it is to assess quality or productivity throughout the system using common indicators of quality for all the providers. An indicator of quality in a doctoral degree program, such as providing students with a context for analytical thinking, may not be a good quality indicator for a course in safety training, where the main objective may be to prevent accidents in the workplace.

State higher education boards are addressing this problem in a variety of ways. Some have chosen to cluster institutions with similar missions. In Tennessee, for example, institutions are divided into three categories: universities/doctoral institutions, two-year institutions, and technical colleges. With such groupings, the state developed indicators appropriate to each group so that institutions can compare themselves with similar institutions. Despite this ability to conduct comparisons, however, Tennessee provides funding by assessing how an institution's performance compares with its own performance in prior years rather than the performance of other institutions in its category. Other state higher education boards allow each institution to determine its own quality indicators. In Kentucky, the Council on Postsecondary Education, for example, concluded that no single definition of quality would work for all institutions in its system: two research universities, six comprehensive universities, and twenty-eight community and technical colleges. Instead of clustering institutions, the council decided to focus on individual "fitness for purpose" as a way for each institution to define its own purpose or mission. This approach allows for the assessment of quality to then focus on individual purposes unique to each institution. This focus is relatively new, and the success of this effort has not been measured.

Although the Council on Postsecondary Education in Kentucky is mainly concerned with public education, it does attempt to ensure the quality of the state's private higher education institutions as well, even though the council does not exercise authority over them. This situation is analogous to the challenges faced by corporations and government agencies that are charged with assessing external contractors who provide educational opportunities for employees.

For systems with great heterogeneity, Model One provides the most flexibility to conduct systemwide assessment. Because Model Three allows the provider to conduct its own assessment, it suits a heterogeneous system but does not include a role for an intermediary to make comparative or system-level assessments. Heterogeneity is not relevant to Model Four, because it focuses on assessing students. Model Two, on the other hand, which puts an external organization in charge of the whole assessment process, is the most problematic approach for heterogeneous systems. As the experience of state boards in Kentucky and Tennessee suggests, accountability assessments must acknowledge that a single set of standards does not suit all institutions. Even some accrediting agencies are modifying their approach so that institutions can develop their own indicators.

## Provider Complexity Within a System

Within a system, individual providers can be more or less complex. Although one provider may simply provide contracted courses, another provider might offer courses, programs, and degrees. In cases where different providers embody differing levels of complexity, it is difficult to determine how to measure the quality and productivity of the multipurpose providers and difficult to compare them with the providers who serve only one purpose.

Models One and Three are well suited to a complex environment because they allow the provider institutions to determine the appropriate level and focus of assessment. Model Two can work in a complex system but requires a substantial amount of advance effort in defining the relevant unit of analysis for each assessment. This process is more challenging in large systems. Model Four is somewhat immune to the level of complexity, because students are assessed with little regard to their providers. Regardless of the model chosen, the assessor may want to spend time defining both the components and the levels of each of the providers that will be assessed.

## Summary

Table 2 summarizes the applicability of different models to the factors discussed in this section, focusing on the purpose of assessment and constraining levels of other factors discussed. (By constraining levels, we mean levels at which certain models are more likely to succeed, such as low level of authority or high level of heterogeneity.) When the level of these characteristics is not

**TABLE 2**
**Suitability of Assessment Models to Different Circumstances**

| Factors | Model 1 | Model 2 | Model 3 | Model 4 |
|---|---|---|---|---|
| Focus on accountability | * | x | | * |
| Focus on improvement | x | | x | * |
| Low level of authority | * | | x | x |
| Constrained resources | * | | x | |
| Little centralization | x | | x | x |
| High system heterogeneity | x | * | x | * |
| High system complexity | x | * | x | * |

x = model likely to be successful

* = model may be successful

constraining (i.e., high level of authority or low heterogeneity), any of the models could be successful.

When a new assessment entity is being established, it is often the case that its approach is not clearly defined at the outset. In such cases, it is advisable for the assessor to consider the context in which it operates and select an approach that is appropriate to its circumstances.

An assessor does not need to adopt a single model for all purposes or all providers. Perhaps competencies could be defined and measured for certain activities or job categories. This use of Model Four could be combined with a version of Model One in which an intermediary evaluates the processes used by some providers to assess their own quality. With other providers, for example those that are already accredited by other intermediaries, an assessor may want them to conduct their own assessments and provide them with helpful information without attempting to evaluate their performance.

# Three Steps for Assessing Providers

REGARDLESS OF THE MODEL chosen for Phase Two, three key steps are involved in the assessment of the quality and productivity of providers of education and professional development: (1) identifying the goals that the education and professional development is designed to accomplish; (2) measuring performance related to those goals; and (3) evaluating performance measures in relation to the established goals (see Palomba and Banta, 1999, for a comprehensive discussion of provider assessment). The three steps used in the assessment of providers is part of Phase Two and is designed to determine whether providers are meeting the needs of their stakeholders.

The literature on education and training assessment is vast. Different sources tend to focus on only a single aspect or step of provider assessment. The information presented in this chapter synthesizes information on provider assessment and, to a lesser extent, student assessment gathered through a review of the literature, interviews, and conference attendance. Using this information, this chapter describes ways in which various institutions set goals, determine measures, and evaluate those measures to ensure that the goals they have set are being met. It summarizes important issues to consider at each step of the process of assessing providers. An important theme that emerged from the literature review is the need to integrate all three steps of the assessment process. Although many organizations and assessment approaches provide useful examples of a single step of the process, such examples are often lacking on how to integrate the three steps. Therefore, after a detailed description of the three steps, a subsection at the end of this chapter describes the balanced scorecard process as an example of how to integrate the three steps.

# Step One: Identify Goals

The first step in assessing providers is to identify the education and professional development goals against which the performance of the provider or, in the case of Model Four, the student will be assessed. The goals should reflect the mission, vision, and values of the assessor and address the question of what the education and professional development is trying to accomplish.

### Setting Goals Guides the Assessment Process

Setting goals sets the stage for the entire assessment. It is important to establish goals before moving on to other assessment endeavors for at least two reasons. First, delineating goals ensures that all the important aspects of the educational endeavor will be assessed. Second, this goal-setting process ensures that extraneous measures will not be created. Unfortunately, the tendency is to ignore this first step and try to determine what can be measured without a framework of goals. Measures may then be chosen that do not necessarily reflect a core value of the assessor. Unfortunately, then, people who must provide data to evaluate the measures will believe these measures to be important; thus, time and effort and other resources may be spent on activities that do not reflect core values. In addition, if assessors connect implications to performance measures, even greater incentives exist for the assessed to focus on performing well on the measure, even if the measure does not reflect the goal of either the assessor or the assessed. Goals and values are therefore inferred from the measures, yet they might not be the goals and values the assessor would have chosen.

> **Setting goals sets the stage for the entire assessment.**

### How to Set Goals

Although the literature we reviewed and the practitioners we interviewed were clear on the importance of first establishing goals, there is no consensus on how to go about this process. Some entities develop goals in response to problems. For example, a state may develop a goal of guarding against fraud after discovering that institutions are misusing student loan funds. Other entities develop goals as part of a strategic planning process. These goals flow from their vision, mission, and values statement. Regardless of how the goals are chosen, two key points should be kept in mind during goal setting. The first is to focus on a manageable number of goals. In undertaking the balanced scorecard approach to assessment, University of Southern California officials stressed that the process of limiting the number of their goals imposed discipline upon the committee and forced committee members to delineate their priorities. Limiting the number of goals keeps the assessment process focused on the values and priorities most important to the assessor. Keeping the number of goals limited also helps to reduce costs. No set number of goals is touted as a rule of thumb, but limiting them is in general a best practice.

### Level of Stakeholder Involvement

The second key point in setting goals is to consider the level of involvement to accord to different stakeholders and the mechanisms for achieving such involvement. In deciding which stakeholders to include in the goal-setting process, the assessor should consider whom the assessment is intended to benefit. Intended beneficiaries should be involved in setting goals. Many provider institutions hold town meetings or focus groups to gather important stakeholders, such as parents, community members, business owners, and government officials, to discern their goals for higher education. If stakeholders are not included in this process, there is no guarantee that the assessment will benefit them. In cases where an intermediary organization controls the assessment process, goal identification becomes more complicated (when the assessor is part of a system, goal identification can overlap with Phase One assessment). Most intermediaries operate at the system level, or even outside the system, so tension can exist between the goals that the providers and stakeholders articulate and what the intermediaries identify as the providers' goals. For example, state higher education boards frequently mediate dramatic disconnects between system- and institution-level goals. At the state level, policymakers are concerned with

**If stakeholders are not included in this process [setting goals], there is no guarantee that the assessment will benefit them.**

issues such as access and equity for the state population as a whole. These concerns, however, may go against what institutional leaders desire for their campuses. An example could be a campus that wants to develop a new program, but the state decides that the program would duplicate efforts at another campus.

Different methods exist for dealing with this tension between intermediary goals and stakeholder/provider goals. Some intermediaries set their own goals for the assessment without regard for the goals of stakeholders or providers. The *U.S. News & World Report* assessment process is the most extreme example of an intermediary that has identified goals with little input from either stakeholders or providers. Not surprisingly, their rankings have been the object of criticism from providers and some customers for failing to account for important dimensions of performance. Nevertheless, *U.S. News & World Report* representatives are satisfied with their process.

Other intermediaries need to involve stakeholders and providers in the goal-setting process. This need typically arises from the necessity of ensuring that the assessment meets the needs of stakeholders. This need can also arise as a result of a lack of authority on the part of the intermediary, however. If the intermediary has little authority, it may gain credibility by acting as a convener for stakeholders and a clearinghouse for their goals. If the intermediary does indeed want to gather stakeholders' input during the goal-setting process, several examples of how to go about it are available from state boards, accrediting associations, and corporations.

**Kentucky State Higher Education Board.** In Kentucky, the current president of the Council on Postsecondary Education (CPE) visited each public higher education institution in the state when he was originally appointed. At the same time, the CPE president conducted focus groups with state citizens to understand their concerns about higher education. CPE and institutional leaders now meet monthly. The meetings keep CPE abreast of institutional concerns and innovations. They also illustrate the "vulnerabilities and alliances" of the institutional leaders. The CPE president uses the meetings to build consensus about institutional goals and priorities.

**Western Association of Schools and Colleges Accrediting Agency.** The Western Association of Schools and Colleges represents a new direction for some accrediting agencies. A new accrediting process is being developed that is based on the individual institutional mission. Therefore, goals on which the assessment process is based reflect each institution's mission rather than a set of accreditation standards applied to every institution. In moving toward this new process, WASC has solicited feedback from several stakeholders. WASC has titled its efforts "Invitation to Dialogue," which aptly captures what it is trying to accomplish. Many different stakeholders have been involved throughout the dialogue process, including a wide range of institutional representatives and other experts on higher education.

**Corporate Learning Organizations.** The approaches used by corporate learning organizations to identify goals for professional development and education display some common features. Typically, learning goals are based on the corporation's strategic plan plus core competencies and other competencies taken as critical to the mission success of the enterprise's several lines of business. The learning goals therefore relate to business goals. Corporations use several methods for involving various constituents in defining these goals. At Lucent, for example, each of fifteen curriculum areas has a business performance council that includes powerful people in the company. More than 160 people are on these councils, including a dean and approximately twenty subject matter experts for each curriculum.

The business performance councils at Lucent are considered stakeholders in education and training in that they are responsible for much more than education and training. They consider all strategic issues related to their particular area, specifically considering education and training as part of the key strategic business issues and setting goals for the education and training that reflect their business needs.

# Step Two: Select Measures

Once the goals for education and professional development activities have been identified, the next step is to develop measures of performance. These measures should be clearly linked to the goals identified in Step One. Linking measures to goals ensures that all goals will be addressed and that extraneous measures will not be developed. Measures can focus on inputs, processes, or outcomes.

## *Input Measures*

**Linking measures to goals ensures that all goals will be addressed and that extraneous measures will not be developed.**

*Inputs* are any resources that are used in the education process, such as the learner's level of knowledge or ability upon enrollment; faculty, technology, or library resources; and dollars spent on curriculum development. Input measures are frequently used in the education, training, and professional development environment. The use of input measures is based on the assumption that more or better inputs generate more or better outcomes. Sometimes a correlation between inputs and outcomes can be established empirically. For example, the American Society for Training and Development benchmarking project found that training expenditures per employee are correlated with company performance; training expenditures per employee has thus gained credibility as a performance measure. Common input measures include education/training expenditures as a percentage of payroll, hours of training per employee per year, percentage of employees trained per year, education/training expenditures per learner, or employee and student characteristics (e.g., standardized test scores).

## *Process Measures*

*Process* is the way in which the education and training is delivered or produced; it differs from the use of the word in the description of Model One in that it refers to the process the provider uses to produce education and professional development. Process measures can include teaching methods, decisions about the content of materials, faculty-student contact, and the number of faculty per student. *Process* also includes more abstract concepts. Does a learning experience involve direct contact with tenured faculty? Does it require students to use critical-thinking skills? Are asynchronous learning techniques used? All these questions relate to the process of education and professional development.

Such process measures are also used frequently, particularly in higher education. Interest is growing in process measures, partly because of the popularity of business models such as total quality management and continuous quality improvement that emphasize the role of production processes in generating better outcomes.

As with input measures, the use of process measures is based on the assumption that certain processes are associated with desired outcomes. In higher education, a useful study linking process to outcomes (see Chickering and Gamson, 1991) identifies processes that produce good student outcomes: student-faculty contact, cooperation among students, active learning, prompt feedback, time on task, high expectations, and respect for diverse talents. Cost per unit output, a typical measure of productivity, is another process measure. When the output produced by the system is diverse (e.g., yearlong courses as well as two-hour seminars), it is useful to use a method that can allow for the aggregation of such heterogeneity. For example, the Lucent Technologies learning organization calculates cost per learner hour, which provides a common denominator that can allow for comparisons between very different types of learning activities (e.g., a weeklong course and an hour-long tutorial).

### Outcome Measures

*Outcomes* reflect both what is produced by education, such as the number of graduates, and the overall impact of the education and professional development.[9] Outcomes typically relate closely to the goals of the education and professional development process. Outcomes can include the impact of the learning experience on the learner's job performance or lifetime income or the acquisition of a specific skill or level of knowledge. Outcome measures are attractive because they can be directly related to goals. Examples of outcome measures used in higher education include passing rate of graduates on licensure exams (by discipline or field), scores on a senior exit exam, employment outcomes, job performance evaluations, and evidence of skills acquired.

As opposed to inputs and processes, which typically describe characteristics of the institution, outcome measures are desirable in that they examine the impact of the institution. Such impacts are typically similar to the institution's goals. For example, an outcome measure (and an institutional goal) may be to graduate a higher percentage of students. Examining outcomes by themselves can provide a good diagnostic tool identifying problems with the education and professional development, but outcome measures alone are limited in their usefulness for proposing solutions to deficiencies. To find such solutions, outcomes should be measured in relation to both inputs and processes so that the assessor can understand the processes that affect outcomes. For example, if pass rates on a specific examination are low, the assessor should relate these rates to the level of preparation of the students upon entry (inputs) and the classes they take and other experiences they have during the educational process (processes).

### Choosing Measures

In choosing measures, it is important to keep five key points in mind. The first is to attempt to develop a mix of input, process, and outcome measures. Although input measures are frequently used as measures of quality in the education, training, and professional development setting, the systems we examined (corporations, states, government agencies) are increasingly emphasizing the use of all three types of measures. The emphasis stems from a desire for valid and reliable evidence of progress toward desired goals. Banta and Borden (1994) compiled a list of specific measures used by institutions of higher education across the country.

> *Input or resource indicators originally received most attention because they were easiest to measure. . . . The 1980s saw a groundswell of interest in the other side of the ledger: outcomes. Following the advent of performance funding in Tennessee, three-quarters of the states adopted policies that caused public colleges and universities to collect and report some kind of outcome information. . . . More recently, Deming and others have caused us to turn our attention to the intervening processes that use resources to produce outcomes. Measuring an outcome will not, in and of itself, result in improvement, they say. We need to examine carefully the processes that lead to outcomes if we hope to improve them [p. 99].*

The second key point is to go beyond readily available measures. In examining measures commonly used to assess higher education at the state level, Richardson (1994) found that states tend to focus on readily available measures. Most states measure enrollment, retention rates, progression rates, and graduation rates. Although collecting these data may indeed allow the states to measure whether they are meeting their goals, it is likely that there are additional goals that cannot be measured without gathering more extensive data.

Recognizing that readily available measures fail to account for important goals, many providers or assessors are undertaking major projects to gather information for alternative measures.

- The Texas Higher Education Coordinating Board has developed the Academic Performance Indicator System. This information system contains longitudinal data on students (demographic information, unique identifiers, course enrollments, and completions), courses (including how many students began and completed the course), and student outcomes (graduation, employment). Students can be tracked across colleges or systems and even into the workforce by linking Social Security numbers to Texas Workforce Commission data. As a result, schools can get a picture of how their graduates do. These data are instrumental in determining whether Texas institutions are meeting goals of student achievement both while in college and after graduation.
- The University of Phoenix staff have developed their own assessment tools to measure whether they are meeting their goals. For example, the Cognitive Outcomes Comprehensive Assessment (COCA) and the Adult Learning Outcomes Assessment (ALOA) are curriculum-specific tests administered to students at the beginning and end of each course to measure what they have learned. The COCA is a cognitive assessment tool, while the ALOA is an affective/behavioral assessment. All the students take the COCA and ALOA as a matriculation and graduation requirement. Examining the scores on these tests allows university staff to determine whether the institution is meeting its goals regarding student achievement, including whether students are learning the skills deemed important in the course objectives. The University of Phoenix also conducts regular surveys

of alumni and employers to ensure that it is meeting its goals of preparing alumni for the workforce.

- The Kirkpatrick model is used in corporate and government settings to assess the quality and productivity of professional development and education. This model recommends the use of several measures for each of four levels described by the model. In the first level, learner satisfaction is measured through the use of course evaluations, satisfaction surveys, and other tools. At the second level, course mastery is assessed through such measures as skill tests, observations, and passing rates. In the third level, job application of the learning is measured through such tools as interviews, focus groups, and managers' ratings of students. Finally, at the fourth level, impact on the organization is measured through the use of such tools as customer satisfaction surveys, customer retention, and continued demand for the education or training (Kirkpatrick, 1998).

A third key point in choosing measures is that although it is important to go beyond readily available measures, developing measures can be expensive, so it is necessary to keep value for cost in mind. A choice faced by assessors in all contexts we examined is how much effort to expend on data collection for the purposes of constructing performance measures. Ultimately, each assessor must grapple with the trade-off between higher cost and better information on how well the provider meets the desired goals. For the University of Phoenix, the costs to develop its homegrown instruments are substantial. It would like to use externally developed tests so that their students could be compared with national norms, but good tests are not available in most of the subject areas needed. Therefore, the university has decided to spend the money for developing its own tests.

The fourth point is that it is important to get feedback from stakeholders on measures if stakeholders will be involved in either gathering or evaluating the measures. One method of getting this feedback is to pilot the measures with a subset of the population. Piloting is typically an effective and efficient way to obtain feedback. Fifth, it is important to develop multiple measures for each goal. Such redundancy helps to ensure that the goal will be validly and reliably measured.

# Step Three: Evaluate Performance Using Measures

In the course of our research, we identified four basic methods used to evaluate performance in the education and professional development context. Each method is based on a comparison involving the measured performance of the provider or student; the methods differ in the basis against which the comparison is made. Four bases of comparison are used: (1) the performance of external peers, (2) preset performance standards, (3) the performance of internal peers, and (4) prior performance of the provider or student. These methods of evaluation are not mutually exclusive; an assessor may combine them for a more comprehensive interpretation of the results. In our review of the literature, we found no evidence supporting the notion that one evaluation method is better than the others (for a history of the use of performance indicators in the United States, see Borden and Bottrill, 1994). Each evaluation method has its own strengths and weaknesses, depending on the circumstances, available data, and existence of internal or external peers. In general, organizations use several evaluation methods, and the four basic evaluation approaches can overlap. In particular, evaluation can be based on objective standards and still involve a comparison with internal or external peers or even with past performance. This approach often occurs, for example, with performance budgeting.[10] Institutional response to such efforts typically depends on what the institution is being asked to do (what data it must submit) and how the data are ultimately used (e.g., does funding depend on performance?). In a survey of campus officials and state policymakers, Serban (1998a) asked respondents which criteria they preferred be used in judging institutional performance: comparisons over time, comparisons with peer institutions, comparisons with targeted external standards, or a combination of all three. Responses indicated that most respondents wanted to be judged using a combination of all three types of criteria.

## *Comparison with External Peers*

One approach to evaluating outcomes is to compare the performance of a provider or a student with the performance of similar external providers or students on the same measures. External benchmarking, as it is commonly called, is a traditional method of evaluation in the case of providers assessing themselves for program improvement and intermediaries assessing education systems for accountability. For example, many state higher education coordinating boards identify peer institutions for each institution in their state and compare performance on that basis. In other cases, institutions themselves identify a set of peer institutions and compare their performance with those peers, normally to promote program improvement. In the Urban Universities Portfolio Project, a group of urban institutions rallied together to form a set of measures relevant to their own unique mission and student bodies (see www.imir.iupui.edu/portfolio for a complete description). In Kentucky, the state as a whole compares itself to other states on some high-level performance measures such as *Kids Count* rankings (which ranks states in terms of how well they foster the welfare of children) and higher education participation rates. The identification of peer groups can increase buy-in from providers, as they will then be compared with institutions similar to their own.

To evaluate measures through comparisons with external peers, three conditions should be met. First, appropriate peer groups must be available. Second, these peers must provide the necessary data. Some organizations rely on third parties to collect data on providers that can then be used by the providers themselves for benchmarking. For example, the American Society for Training and Development (http://www.astd.org/) collects input and process measures associated with performance improvements from a group of organizations known for their best practices. The National Association of College and University Business Officers engages in a similar practice with data from higher education institutions (http://nacubo.eduprise.com/courses/resource/HEAP-EPDWatlib.nsf). Availability of data is an important factor in determining the feasibility of external benchmarking, as it requires providers or third parties to consistently and honestly report information on the criteria of interest, which brings us to the third point. Assessors must be able to trust the data provided by peers. *U.S. News & World Report* rankings, a clear example of the use of external benchmarking for evaluation, has faced criticism regarding the reliability of information (particularly the self-report information) used to develop the rankings. As the rankings have grown more popular in the public eye, institutions have a greater incentive to provide erroneous information.

## Comparison with Preset Standards

A second evaluation method is to compare performance with preset standards. Some state higher education coordinating boards use this evaluation approach in preparing report cards on each institution that rank how well the institution has done in comparison with preset standards, such as rates for enrollment, retention, and graduation. The report cards can also include measures of student learning, academic programs (i.e., program accreditation), faculty productivity, and financial accountability. The Tennessee and South Carolina report card systems set specific performance targets for different types of institutions (see http://www.tbr.state.tn.us/research/reportcard/reportcard99.htm and http://www.che400.state.sc.us/web/Perform/IE/IEPage.htm for more information about each state's reporting requirements). Indeed, as discussed earlier, a challenge that assessors face as they try to evaluate a heterogeneous group of providers is setting standards appropriate to different types of providers.

One limitation of using preset criteria is that they can stifle any incentive to perform at a level above the criteria. Moreover, if the result of such an evaluation is simply whether or not the institution met the criteria, then this approach will not allow stakeholders to distinguish among providers. This criticism is leveled against the accreditation process, which traditionally compares an institution's performance measures with preset criteria required for accreditation. In addition, comparison with preset standards is typically geared toward accountability rather than improvement, which is less palatable to the institutions being assessed.

> **One limitation of using preset criteria is that they can stifle any incentive to perform at a level above the criteria.**

## Comparison with Internal Peers

Another method for evaluating measures is to compare performance with that of internal peers. This approach is used in education in situations where internal peers are available, such as within a multicampus institution or a multi-institution system. For example, as part of its assessment process, the University of Phoenix benchmarks the performance of 65 different sites against one another, using a broad portfolio of assessment practices that enables it to compare both the quality of curriculum and the quality of administrative practices among the different sites. Campuses are not graded or penalized for poor performance, but they are compared with one another. The incentive structure attempts to link rewards to outcomes.

### Comparison with Past Performance

Last, organizations can compare themselves with their prior performances. This method is referred to as *historical benchmarking*. In such cases, organizations generate baseline data and compare past with present performance: where were we in terms of quality and productivity, and where are we now? Normally, the evaluation centers on whether performance is improving. Institutions may prefer this approach, because they are compared with themselves rather than with other institutions that they consider dissimilar and because the focus is geared toward improvement rather than accountability.

This method is extremely common because it does not require the entity to identify peers or to gather external data. It is relatively easy to collect and track the same information on a single provider or student over time, especially as organizations install suitable information systems. For example, the Learning and Development unit at Lucent Technologies closely tracks the cost per learner hour and compares it with past performance on that dimension. Lucent has reduced that cost by 50 percent and views it as a major success. Serban (1998b) reports that Tennessee, Missouri, Ohio, Kentucky, Minnesota, Washington, and Arkansas have used historical comparisons to determine whether institutions in the state are improving (all but Missouri used peer comparisons or preset targets as well).

An important limitation of historical benchmarking is that it lacks an external perspective. Performance may be improving, but was the baseline bad or good? Is the improvement occurring quickly enough? For this reason, historical benchmarking is often paired with external benchmarking.

# Measurement Validity and Reliability

In establishing goals, choosing measures, and evaluating these measures, it is important to consider issues of validity and reliability. In other words, does the assessment process accurately capture what it intends to capture? Validity and reliability concern whether measures as designed and administered provide good estimates of the concept under investigation (see, e.g., American Psychological Association, 1985; Babbie, 1992; Campbell and Fiske, 1959; Campbell and Stanley, 1966; H. Cole and others, 1984; Cook and Campbell, 1979; Cronbach, 1971; Cronbach and Gleser, 1965; Dickinson and Hedge, 1989; Light, Singer, and Willett, 1990; Messick, 1975, 1989, Messick, 1996; Nunnally, 1970; Singleton, Straits, and Miller Straits, 1993; Snow, 1974; Tannenbaum and Yukl, 1992; Thorndike, 1971; Winer, 1971). Most of the literature in this area relates to valid and reliable measures of learning. In other words, researchers are interested in whether the tests used to ascertain student learning are valid and reliable. The concepts of and challenges to validity and reliability discussed here also pertain to other types of measures, however. Although the issues of measurement validity and reliability appear to relate primarily to Step Two of the assessment process (selecting measures), they are, in fact, important concepts to consider in all three steps.

Several techniques can be used to ensure both validity and reliability. Four of these techniques are presented here and all are relevant to assessment steps one through three: (1) the continued solicitation of expert feedback; (2) extensive piloting of the measures with members of the target population before use; (3) use of multiple measures to evaluate the underlying construct; and (4) comparison of results of measures used with results of other measures and tests for similar groups over time.

During Step One, as goals are defined, feedback should be solicited from appropriate stakeholders, including those who will be involved in judging whether the objectives are met. During Step Two, as measures are chosen, feedback should be solicited from stakeholders to ensure that objectives have been realistically represented. In developing these measures, the assessor should ensure that multiple measures are used for each goal. Once measures have been developed, they should be piloted with a subset of the intended population. In Step Three, when these measures are evaluated, they should be evaluated as stand-alone measures but also compared, to the extent possible, with other preexisting measures. These actions may not ensure validity and reliability, but they are good steps in that direction.

# Bringing It All Together: Integrating All Three Steps

Although the literature review and case studies provide concrete information on each step, few examples are available for guiding an intermediary in integrating all three steps. The balanced scorecard, however, provides a useful framework for such integration. It is a framework that has been adopted as a strategic management system by a wide range of organizations, including corporations, universities, nonprofit organizations, and government agencies (see Appendix D). It is designed to help organizations translate their vision and mission statements into performance goals, while taking into account multiple perspectives, including those of customers, internal constituents, and providers of the education or training. The balanced scorecard is used primarily by provider organizations to identify goals and then translate those goals into operational performance measures.

The balanced scorecard is based on four main processes: translating the vision, communication and alignment, business planning, and feedback and learning. All four processes aim to create consistency and integrate priorities across the organization and to determine the right performance measures. The translation of the vision is meant to create an understanding of the organization's vision through an "integrated set of objectives and measures, agreed upon by all senior executives, that describe the long-term drivers of success" (Kaplan and Norton, 1996, p. 76). The vision and strategy should then be communicated throughout the organization to ensure that departmental and individual employee goals are properly aligned with the long-term strategic vision. The business planning aspect links the budget to strategic planning and performance measurement, allowing decision makers to direct resources appropriately. Finally, the feedback and learning mechanism provides an opportunity for decision makers to review performance results and assess the validity of the organization's strategy and performance measures. The balanced scorecard emphasizes continually updating strategy and measures to accurately reflect the changing operating environment.

The balanced scorecard allows the provider to include as many stakeholders as necessary in the determination of goals. The scope and number of goals are flexible in that they can change as the operating environment of the institution changes, although it is suggested that the number of goals in each perspective area be limited to a handful. According to University of Southern California officials, who use the balanced scorecard approach in the School of Education, the process of limiting the number of their goals imposed discipline on the committee and forced members to delineate their priorities. Furthermore, the balanced scorecard framework encourages institutions to identify a limited number of measures that relate to the goals they have established.

In this process, evaluation of the measures relies on the comparison of performance with that of external peers (benchmarking). Indeed, the need to benchmark and the availability of such benchmarking information influences the choice of performance measures. The purpose of the balanced scorecard is for managers to select indicators that can help them monitor progress toward a few key goals. Table 3 provides examples of the University of Southern California's goals, measures, and benchmarks used in its balanced scorecard assessment process.

## Relevance of the Three Assessment Steps to Assessors

Our description of the three principal steps of assessment highlights several points. First, the steps should be followed in order. In particular, it is crucial to avoid selecting measures *before* or *without* defining goals. Practitioners in higher education, corporate, and government agency settings stressed the tendency of individuals to value or emphasize what is measured and divert attention toward it. Therefore, it is important for assessors to be sure that the measures they are examining are tightly related to key goals.

In determining goals, it is important to reach consensus on a manageable number of goals. In addition, the assessor should consider which stakeholders and providers to include in this process for determining goals. Generally, the assessment process should include all the stakeholders and providers who are intended to benefit from the assessment. In other words, if a stakeholder such as an employer of graduates is intended to benefit from the assessment, this employer should be included in setting goals for the assessment. Including

**TABLE 3**
**University of Southern California School of Education Goals,**
**Measures, and Benchmarks**

| Goal | Measure | Benchmark |
|---|---|---|
| Quality of academic programs | Ranking in *U.S. News & World Report* | Ascend to top 10 schools of education |
| | Teaching effectiveness | Equal average of top 5 USC schools |
| Student-centeredness | Quality of student services measured by student satisfaction with advisement, career development, job placement, course offerings, financial aid, etc.; school climate for special population students (international, minority, women) | |
| Quality of faculty | Publications | Exceed average of publications per USC tenure-track faculty member |
| | Research funding | Equal average of top 11–20 in *U.S. News & World Report* |
| Value for money | Retention | Equal average of top 5 of USC graduate programs |
| | Reduced time to degree | Reduce time by 20 percent |
| | Return on student investment | Break even |
| Alumni satisfaction | To be developed | |
| Employer satisfaction | Quality of elementary and secondary school teachers | |

*Source:* O'Neil, Bensimon, Diamond, and Moore, 1999, p. 37.

such stakeholders should have the added benefit of increasing the legitimacy of the assessor. There are several ways to solicit such input, including meetings, visits, focus groups, and establishing boards or committees.

In terms of selecting measures, the assessor should ensure that the measures flow from the chosen goals. Within this constraint, it should ensure that the measures chosen reflect input, process, and outcome measures, going beyond readily available measures to ensure that there are valid and reliable measures for each goal. Choosing multiple measures for each goal helps to ensure reliability and validity. Throughout this process, it is important to consider value for cost, because much of this work is quite expensive. Finally, when multiple measures reflecting inputs, processes, and outcomes have been chosen for each goal, the assessor should consider piloting these measures with a subset of the institution's population to ensure that they will work for the institution's purposes.

**Establishing a regular cycle and process for determining goals helps to ensure that goals reflect current needs.**

When it comes to evaluating performance, the assessor has four methods to choose from: comparing performance of the measures with (1) external peers, (2) preset standards, (3) internal peers, and (4) prior performance. All of these evaluation techniques should be considered for each measure, and combining more than one technique is encouraged. Multiple methods of evaluation help to ensure the reliability and validity of the measures.

One final lesson from this section is that many organizations continually and regularly reconsider each of the three steps in the assessment process. Establishing a regular cycle and process for determining goals helps to ensure that goals reflect current needs. This process can be formal or informal.

# Conclusions and Recommendations

THIS REPORT HAS PROVIDED a broad overview of the variety of approaches used in different systems to assess the quality and productivity of education, training, and professional development. This overview is valuable because it draws together and identifies commonalities among the vast array of assessment activities. In presenting this overview, we have developed a scheme for classifying assessment approaches that distinguishes different stages of the process and distills common features among seemingly different assessment activities. Such an overview should be useful to any organization that is developing from scratch or refining an educational assessment activity.

First, we distinguished between the high-level assessment of whether the set of educational providers is meeting the needs of the system as a whole (Phase One) and the more narrow assessment of whether providers are meeting the needs of their current stakeholders (Phase Two). We subsequently categorized the approaches of Phase Two assessment into four types (Models One to Four) and described the strengths and weaknesses of those models.

**The details of an assessment process are often specific to the context in which the assessment is to occur.**

An important lesson drawn from this review is that the details of an assessment process are often specific to the context in which the assessment is to occur. Our review did highlight some general lessons for assessors, however, regardless of the context.

# Phase One Recommendations

Education and professional development activities, as we have defined them in this report, are normally part of larger systems with a mission that goes well beyond education and training. A clear trend in each of these systems we considered (states, corporations, and government agencies) is the development of a learning organization that is responsible for more than just the assessment of existing providers. Rather, these organizations play a key role in promoting communication among stakeholders and developing a clear link among education, training, and professional development on the one hand and the basic mission of the system on the other. Corporate learning organizations describe this role as becoming a strategic partner in the corporation. Part of this function is often to convince customer organizations that learning is important.

This strategic role is crucial to the assessment process, as it ensures that the goals on which provider-level (Phase Two) assessment is based are consistent with the goals of the system as a whole. In particular, it can help ensure that the needs of all stakeholders are at least being considered (if not addressed). Phase One assessment can also ensure that activities important to the system as a whole but not necessarily to individual parts of the system (such as leadership training in a corporation) receive adequate consideration in the assessment process. Phase One assessment can also contribute to the effective use of resources across the system. In general, education and professional development is a means to an end rather than an end in and of itself. For this reason, education systems constantly compete for resources with other activities in corporations, government agencies, and states.

# Phase Two Recommendations

This report presents four models for Phase Two assessment, which examines the quality of existing providers or the skills acquired by learners. We found no clear evidence that one assessment approach is unequivocally more effective than others in ensuring quality. Each model has strengths and weaknesses, many of which depend on the specific context of the system and of the organization in charge of the assessment. We emphasize that an assessor does not need to choose a single model for all purposes or providers. For example, Model Four might be useful for specific groups of learners who are acquiring well defined job-related competencies. Model Three might be useful for institutions that are already accredited by regional accrediting agencies. Model One or Two might be useful for institutions that are not otherwise accredited.

Indeed, an important challenge facing assessors responsible for assessing heterogeneous education and professional development activities might be grouping those activities in a consistent manner and applying different models to different groups. The model selected must be a good match for the provider's activities, the assessor's purpose, and the nature of the relationship between the provider and assessor.

### Consider the Purpose of Assessment

As this report has discussed, different assessment models have relative strengths and weaknesses related to the purpose of assessment. As a result, it is important for assessors to carefully consider the purpose of the assessment efforts. Is it to promote improvement within provider institutions? Is it to hold institutions accountable to stakeholders' needs? Is it to fix a specific perceived problem? If accountability is an important purpose, then Model Two is the most effective approach, although Models One and Four could also work. On the other hand, if improvement is the aim, then Models One and Three are most likely to succeed. Model One appears to have the best chance of promoting both improvement and accountability.

### Consider Constraints Within the System

The models we describe differ in how well they address different constraints affecting how organizations operate. There is no one-size-fits-all solution. Instead, the assessment approach depends on the constraints and opportunities existing within the system. Many organizations operate within heterogeneous and complex systems. Organizations in such circumstances would be best served by Model One, which offers clear advantages for the second phase of assessment. Model One delegates to the provider organizations the task of defining goals, measuring outcomes, and evaluating outcomes. As a result, Model One can be more easily applied to diverse providers in a system with a low level of authority and little centralization. The primary disadvantage of Model One is that it does not, on the face of it, provide accountability. Implementation of the academic audit, an example of Model One, however, suggests that the model is flexible and could be easily modified to provide for accountability. For example, an organization could develop an audit process that places restrictions on the goals that are deemed appropriate and the type of evidence that can be used to support claims of quality and productivity. The audit process could also be modified to explicitly request certain information.

If the organization were to adopt Model One, it would need to design the auditing process, disseminate results (including best practice reports), and modify the process over time. The organization could audit not only institutions within its own system but also programs and contractor-provided education and professional development outside its system. The audits themselves could be conducted by internal staff or by committees made up of external experts. Again, effort would be required to design and implement a governance structure for assessment. The design of an audit procedure would require some knowledge of existing assessment efforts in institutions and programs.

### *Integrate the Three Assessment Steps*

In terms of the process used to assess providers, this report has emphasized that there are three key steps involved in that process: identifying goals, measuring outcomes, and evaluating outcomes in relation to goals. Linking measures and evaluation to goals is a clear best practice used by all sorts of providers in many contexts. The balanced scorecard provides a useful framework for linking the three steps.

Our literature review also suggests the importance of limiting the number of goals driving the assessment process, selecting process and outcome measures in addition to input measures, and going beyond readily available measures and choosing multiple measures to ensure that valid and reliable measures exist for each goal.

In evaluating the measures, an assessor has four methods of comparing performance measures to choose from: with those of external peers, preset standards, those of internal peers, and prior performance. All these evaluation techniques should be considered for each measure; combining more than one technique is encouraged. Multiple methods of evaluation also help to ensure the reliability and validity of the measures.

# Appendix A: Corporate Professional Development and Training

O UR LITERATURE REVIEW on this topic includes material drawn from best-practice human resource departments and corporate learning organizations as well as corporate universities.[11] Throughout this appendix, we use the term "corporate learning organization" to reflect a high-level commitment to employee learning and a systems-based approach to providing for it, including a corporate university. Corporate learning organizations can be, but are not necessarily, associated with specific physical facilities.

The corporate learning organization can represent an intermediary-aided approach to professional development and education, although many corporate learning organizations have some sort of provider role. Corporate learning organizations typically engage in Phase One system-level assessment activities; however, the structure of Phase Two functions often varies depending on the organization. Examples of Models One, Two, and Three can be found throughout different corporate settings. In corporate America, there is a growing interest in the role of the learning organization as an information gatherer and processor, knowledge broker, and information clearinghouse, in addition to the role of developer and provider of content. The trend appears to be toward increased emphasis on the intermediary role and less emphasis on the provider role.

The intermediary organization, whether it is officially a corporate university or an in-house human resources unit, is increasingly likely to be headed by an individual whose title is "chief learning officer" (CLO). Learning organizations are emphasizing their role as corporate-level partners and the importance of establishing learning as a strategic part of the future of the company, rather than a cost center. Formerly, training was controlled by individual lines of business and each had its own training activities to meet specific needs. Now, the issue of training is being elevated to the corporate level, and activities are being consolidated and rationalized in the interest of both quality and efficiency. This is similar to the transition that information technology went through in the 1980s, when the term "chief information officer" was relatively new. Learning organizations have recognized the importance of getting buy-in from both the CEO and the lines of business in support of their efforts. Many are using "account management" to track the needs of the stakeholders, emphasizing communication and responsiveness. Learning goals must be tied clearly to business goals. Because human resource departments are often held in low esteem in large corporations, learning organizations are often advised to avoid "HR speak" and learn to communicate effectively with the business units.

Corporate learning organizations provide a range of services that are ultimately designed to promote workforce improvement. The intermediary role includes helping employees develop individual learning plans to meet their training needs as well as keeping track of their training needs and accomplishments. To this end, some learning organizations, such as the one at Sun Microsystems, have introduced information "portals" that organize information functionally and allow employees to easily find what they need about learning opportunities throughout the company. United Airlines provides another example. Its central unit responsible for leadership training is developing an interactive Web site that includes online assessments to help an employee determine the skills (math, verbal, and leadership) he or she is lacking. The Web site is a huge information clearinghouse, organized on the basis of the assessments and other information for the benefit of the user. For example, the learner can pull up a list of learning opportunities, both internal and external, that are available through United. Using well-developed web tools, learning organizations can connect and coordinate learning experiences for employees.

In the corporate learning environment, customers are broadly construed to include both learners (employees at all levels of the organization) and managers of the line units whose employees receive education or training. Often intact teams or entire units are engaged in the learning experience. Further, there is increasing interest in including other members or components of the value chain as learners (e.g., suppliers or customers of the line unit, and occasionally collateral units). Such efforts reflect a systems-based approach to learning.

Providers of training, education, and professional development in the corporate setting are a diverse collection of individuals and organizations whose activities are carried out in close collaboration with the intermediary unit. Providers include nonprofit educational institutions (especially if they are flexible about customizing or tailoring coursework and schedules) and for-profit training firms. Frequently, line managers and even senior managers in the organization are also being asked to serve as educators, with assistance from the intermediary unit. In addition, companies develop and deliver their own course material. As a first step, the intermediary must identify the appropriate delivery mechanism and provider. Partnering with existing educational institutions is highly desirable because courses and programs are likely to be accredited or certified; on the other hand, they may have less flexibility and motivation to adapt their procedures to the needs of corporations than would private, for-profit training firms. Learning organizations may elect to develop their own courses. In any case, the intermediary must constantly broker, monitor, and manage relationships between providers and customers of professional development and education. The intermediary must also work with customers and providers to develop learning evaluations.

In spite of all the interest in new technologies for education delivery, many providers still rely on classroom-based instruction. Based on the learning pyramid from National Training Laboratories, popular opinion about the relationship between information retention and education delivery methods posits that students retain 5 percent from lecture, 10 percent from reading, 20 percent from audio-visual aids, 30 percent from demonstration, 50 percent from discussion, 75 percent from practice by doing, and 90 percent from teaching others. Interestingly, while this belief is widely held, no data support the numbers.

In terms of assessment, the human resource office, corporate university, or corporate learning officer is responsible for designing or guiding the assessment, and potentially for implementing or helping to implement it. The intermediary will also take the lead in using assessment results to revise course offerings and give improvement-oriented feedback to providers.

Ultimately, attention to the quality and productivity of professional development and educational activities is motivated by interest in promoting the long-term health and competitiveness of the corporation. However, while the benefits to the corporation are the clear driver, assessment often benefits the employee learners as well. For example, academic accreditation and professional certification are taken by corporations as marks of the quality of courses offered, but corporations also believe it is beneficial to employees to have such accomplishments on their records. Achievement in externally validated courses, they believe, helps ensure lifetime employability in a period when corporations can no longer promise lifetime employment.

Although the reviewed literature reflected a highly diverse collection of businesses and industries, a number of common assumptions underlie and drive their concern for quality and productivity in professional development and education. One dominant theme, for example, is knowledge work as an ever increasing proportion of the total work of organizations. In the United States, as in most developed economies, firms' core competencies are being defined in the context of information-intensive activities. Key corollaries of this theme are systematically increasing skill requirements for most jobs (to produce value-added, knowledge-based goods and services) and continuous learning needs related to technological advance (since information-intensive tasks are highly technology-dependent).

A second major theme in the literature has to do with corporate restructuring. Downsizing and other business process redesign efforts have reshaped organizations, making them flatter, leaner, and more competitive. As a consequence, today's employees are expected to work "smarter"—to become effective self-managers and problem solvers. Emerging interest in knowledge management and intellectual capital suggests that firms are giving more attention to the value of their human resources.

Emphasis on high-performance work systems throughout the value chain is a third noteworthy theme. Line business units in organizations are being asked to reexamine their roles, align their processes with mission-critical enterprise goals, and demonstrate measurable results from their performance improvement strategies. Corporate professional-development functions are experiencing these same pressures.

Taken together, these cross-cutting trends appear to have greatly increased the importance of workplace learning in the corporate literature we reviewed. The growth of corporate universities—from about 400 in 1990 to an estimated 1,000 or more today—signals renewed interest in professional development and education.

As learning and knowledge management become increasingly important to organizations, the value of the learning organization as a strategic partner in the continuous improvement of business processes is emerging as an important trend. Quality assessment results are expected to be useful both for improving learning processes and providing insights on factors that affect organizational performance.

At the employee level, student assessment results are sometimes fed into performance reviews and future career path plans. The literature recommends employee incentives for learning as a way of linking employees' individual goals to organizational performance improvement goals.

Finally, corporate universities and corporate learning units are increasingly being expected to operate on a fee-for-service basis, recovering their operating costs from business units that supply them with customers (learners). Thus they have a strong incentive to monitor their productivity; and it is in their best interests as well to gather and disseminate quality evaluations to potential customer units.

# Phase One

Details of corporate university approaches to identifying goals for professional development and education vary in a number of firm-specific ways. However, they display some common systems-level features. Typically, the learning goals are based on the corporation's strategic plan, plus core and other competencies taken as critical to the mission success of the enterprise's several lines of business.

The intermediary organization is often responsible for setting out the top-level goals for professional development and education activities but must act entrepreneurially to sell the learning agenda within the corporation. It is crucial to enlist strong and visible commitment and support from the corporation's CEO—if the CEO was not a prime mover in creating the corporate university or CLO position. Often, but not always, these learning initiatives are driven from the top. Additionally, it is critical to convince key managers in all lines of business that intellectual capital investment is necessary for survival and success in the current economic environment.

The intermediary's role in goal identification and needs analysis differs among learning organizations. In some cases, learning organizations are responsible for both goal identification and needs analysis to determine in which key areas education and professional-development efforts should be directed. At Sun Microsystems, for example, a framework was developed that can be applied to individual lines of business for identifying goals and establishing where needs exist. For each line of business, the Sun Microsystems corporate university focuses on knowledge management to establish what learners know, competency management to determine what learners need to know, and performance management to help learners use what they know. The Grainger, Inc., learning center has adopted a more bottom-up approach to goal identification. By taking an inventory of the training and education activities going on in the company, they have identified 108 "learning solutions" or training modules and have developed a core curriculum that encompasses twenty-seven of those learning solutions. The core consists of four areas: leadership and management, quality, sales and customer contact, and "digital Grainger." Other learning organizations, such as the United Airlines leadership training unit, have their goals established by corporate headquarters and focus on needs analysis. The training unit has built the curriculum for leadership development around the corporate goals and corporate definition of good leadership and considers its core competency to be needs analysis based on that definition.

A common strategy for selling the learning agenda within the company is to create a governance structure for the corporate university that puts representative managers for primary lines of business on a board of trustees or board of advisors. This structure creates direct formal links between the business units and the intermediary organization and allows business units to help determine the learning goals.

Productivity improvements in professional development and education, in contrast, are often sought to make two main types of changes to the corporate university or corporate learning effort: reorganizations that decrease the administrative costs associated with providing these programs, and innovative uses of information and communication technologies to create more efficient ways of delivering them.

# Phase Two

Many corporate learning organizations are moving toward a lesser role in the actual provision of education and training and a greater role in third-party assessment, following the Model Two structure where the intermediary assesses the quality and productivity of outside providers. It is still common, however, for the corporate learning organization to be both the provider and the assessor. In such cases, the corporate learning organization uses a Model Three approach in its Phase Two activities (e.g., Lucent; see Appendix A1). Finally, some corporate learning organizations serve as advisors to corporate business units that are providing their own training. In this capacity, the corporate learning organizations assume a modified version of Model Three where they make recommendations and guide provider-based assessment.

### *Identify Goals for Education and Training*

The intermediary works with major stakeholder groups to jointly articulate more specific goals and objectives for the varied business lines or directions that professional development and education will take. Subsequently, the intermediary designs curricula in collaboration with customers and providers. Customization aims at developing curricula that will boost the customer unit's successful performance (as determined by the unit's role in the corporate business strategy). Tailoring curricula is considered important for assuring that courses directly address firm-specific and unit-specific performance goals and also for helping to reconcile provider schedules (e.g., academic terms) with customer schedules (e.g., fiscal cycles). In other words, the goals relate mainly to business outcomes.

### *Develop Measures of Quality and Productivity*

Corporate mission goals and objectives typically form the basis for assessment procedures, which must be designed to reflect performance outcomes that are desirable in light of the corporation's strategic plans and the role that employee professional development and education plays in them.

Our review of corporate literature revealed a variety of measures in use for assessment purposes. In general, in the reviewed literature, productivity assessment received far less attention than quality assessment. The productivity assessments we found are generally based on inputs, assuming that outcome quality remains constant. Common examples of productivity measures in use include

- The number of instructional days provided per unit of cost
- The total cost to deliver a course, per student
- The total time required to complete a course, per student.

As noted, these tend to be input measures. The unit of analysis for productivity measures is generally the learning organization or provider of the education.

In contrast, most of the specific measures of quality we found reflect processes or outcomes; their relationship to business performance goals and objectives is generally highly inferential. Because this project emphasizes academic quality over productivity, we identified a number of examples in the corporate literature for several categories of quality measures. The unit of analysis for quality measures can be the business units, the educational providers, or the students.

Input measures are sometimes used as quality metrics in the corporate training environment. From a quality perspective, the underlying assumption is that more inputs generate better or more outcomes. Common input measures include

- Education/training expenditures as a percentage of payroll
- Hours of training per employee per year
- Percentage of employees trained per year
- Education/training expenditures per employee
- Ratio of employees to trainers.

Such external certification as the accreditation or certification of courses is sometimes used as a measure of quality. Organizations may also choose to participate in outside certification of unit processes or recognition of performance (e.g., ISO or Baldrige Award) as a way of determining quality.

Measurement of the quality of professional development and education in the corporate sector continues to rely heavily on the Kirkpatrick framework, which consists of four levels of assessment. The first level is reaction, or trainee satisfaction with the course. The second level is learning and measures how well participants have mastered the course material. Level three is transfer to the job, or how the learning and development is being used on the job. The fourth level is organizational effects and measures changes in the business process itself.

Table A1 summarizes the four Kirkpatrick levels and provides examples of measures used at each level. There is currently a strong emphasis on levels 3 and 4 in corporate professional development and education. However, in practice, most assessment is still being done at level 1, with some assessment at level 2. While many learning organizations consider assessment at levels 3 and 4 to be desirable, they are not able to carry it out in most cases. The value chain has been incorporated into how Kirkpatrick levels 3 and 4 are understood and operationalized. It is regarded, however, as quite difficult and costly to obtain quantifiable measures of performance improvements at levels 3 and 4 and to associate such changes with bottom-line improvements.[12] For instance, Motorola's rigorous effort to estimate the return on its investment in education and training is rumored to have cost over $1 million.

Despite its widespread use, the framework has several limitations. First, it focuses on student learning, which is an important goal of education and professional development, but may not be the only goal of interest to an assessor. Second, what little empirical research exists on Kirkpatrick's typology of measures provides weak evidence of correlation among levels 2–4 and no evidence that level 1 outcomes are related to the others (see Tannenbaum and Yukl, 1992). As noted, levels 1 and 2 are the most commonly used measurements because of their low cost and ease of administration. However, business organizations are generally less interested in individual-level measures of course satisfaction and learning than in the effects of the education and development

**TABLE A1**
**Kirkpatrick Model**

| Kirkpatrick Level | What It Measures | Examples of Measures |
|---|---|---|
| 1. Reaction | Learner satisfaction with course, other aspects of the learner's experience | Course/instructor evaluation<br>Employee job satisfaction survey<br>Employee (pre/post) self-assessment |
| 2. Learning | How well participants have mastered the course material | Technical skill test (pre/post)<br>Observation of standardized task performance (post only)<br>Retention tests |
| 3. Transfer to the job | How learning and development is being used on the job | Qualitative interviews with the learner<br>Focus groups with managers of learners<br>Improvement ratings collected from managers<br>Direct measurement of employee performance (e.g., reduced time-to-completion of tasks) |
| 4. Organizational effects | Effects on the business process itself | Number of defective parts<br>Satisfied-customer index<br>Customer retention<br>Return on investment<br>Return on expectations, where expectations are indicators of valued performance derived and operationalized collaboratively from missions and goals<br>Demand for education/training as a measure of its quality and relevance<br>Desired effects on organizational culture (ethnographic studies pre/post). |

activities on job performance and business processes. Using level 1 or level 2 measures as proxies for higher-level outcomes, such as task or process improvements, is not appropriate and may lead to flawed conclusions.

Some learning organizations have undertaken return-on-investment (ROI) evaluation to underscore the effects of investments in learning and development on a company's productivity. By measuring increases in productivity as a result of education and professional development, the activities of the learning organization are elevated to the level of importance comparable to other strategic investments. The process of ROI evaluation facilitates better management of these activities and promotes their continuous improvement. It is not, however, a viable method of self- or budgetary justification (Bassi, 2000). ROI measurement involves determining the intended business result, establishing the causal relationship between learning and development activities and the result, quantifying the value of that result, identifying metrics, and evaluation. Measurement of the three categories of provision costs is critical for a credible ROI evaluation: direct costs, including payments to vendors and materials; indirect costs, including overhead; and opportunity costs, such as lost productivity (Bassi, 2000). Establishing causal links between learning and development efforts and ROI effects (or other organizational performance effects) is likely to be another difficult step toward the credibility of level 4 evaluation efforts.

While some learning organizations emphasize the importance of ROI assessment (e.g., United Airlines) or an ability to demonstrate the value to the firm, others are moving away from this type of measurement. For example, Cisco focuses instead on the effect of training on the revenue stream. They claim that this is a more "strategic" focus (as opposed to a cost center perspective).

### Evaluate Quality and Productivity Using Measures

As explained earlier, productivity assessments typically turn on input measures, assuming quality of output is held constant. Using these measures, productivity is then evaluated by comparing an organization's current resource-to-output ratio with a prior baseline rate; such methods have been used, for instance, to evaluate whether the introduction of network-based distance learning techniques for a particular course of instruction yields productivity improvements. Alternatively, productivity can be evaluated by comparing the productivity of an organization's education or training activities with those of a benchmark organization. Use of benchmarks for productivity evaluation is dependent on finding appropriate organizations and courses for comparison; this approach is most successful when organizations use similar techniques for determining costs and where equivalence of outputs can readily be established (e.g., for certain kinds of technical training).

Additionally, corporate universities also rely on benchmarking (comparison to leading-edge peers) and standards (e.g., accreditation or certification) in quality evaluations. At least two objectives are served by accreditation or certification of courses. On the one hand, such processes provide the corporate university with an independent and objective evaluation of the quality of specific courses or programs. On the other hand, having taken accredited or certified courses gives employees a portable credential; given that companies cannot promise lifetime employment, they are attempting instead to provide lifetime employability. In return, companies say, they are able to attract and retain better workers.

Benchmarking as a tool for quality evaluation is a widely accepted and familiar practice in the corporate world and was readily extended to serve needs for evaluating the quality of professional development and education. But it is recommended with some caveats: Processes closely linked to performance improvements in one company might not have the same relationship to performance in another; and in any case, benchmarked processes probably need to be tailored to particular contexts rather than adopted as is.

Typically, performance measures of the effects of professional development and education on the performance of units, lines of business, and/or the entire enterprise are evaluated in one of two ways. One involves examining face-valid indicators of performance improvements (indices based, for instance, on defined mission objectives); corporations rarely invest the time and funds necessary to establish the predictive validity of these measures or to link them directly with ROI. An alternative is to rely for evaluative purposes on measures of processes that have been independently benchmarked to performance improvements (e.g., the American Society for Training and Development has defined a set of input and process measures associated with performance improvements in a set of best-practice organizations).

Apart from consortia that establish procedures for collecting and sharing data for benchmarking purposes, evaluation information is not widely shared; typically consortium members hold the information as confidential or proprietary to the association.

Although assessments need to be specific to courses and to business processes, the intermediary organization is expected to establish general evaluation standards and procedures and to ensure their implementation.

# Appendix A1: Lucent Technologies Learning and Performance Center[13]

L UCENT TECHNOLOGIES IS a spin-off from AT&T, specializing in telecommunications equipment. This description was written in the spring of 2000. At this time, the company is moving away from routine manufacturing and concentrating more on high-end manufacturing and telecommunications technologies. It has about 150,000 employees, 45,000 of whom work outside the United States in 67 different countries. Lucent's annual revenue is about $38 billion.

Education, development, and training activities at Lucent occur throughout the entire corporation and are budgeted at about $225 million per year. Much of this activity occurs under or is guided by the Learning and Performance Center (LPC). While the LPC performs the functions of a corporate university—namely, designing and delivering learning opportunities—it also serves a broader function as the leader of the Lucent learning network. The LPC was established in 1996 and currently provides 250,000 learning days per year with a budget of $70 million. Twenty-five percent of the budget comes directly from a corporate allocation, and the remainder comes from tuition charged to the business units that use the training. About 25 percent of the learning days are delivered using technology. The primary purposes of establishing the LPC were to improve content and delivery, reduce costs, and eliminate redundancies.[14]

The LPC has many roles. It monitors both stakeholder and system needs for education and professional development, and it assesses whether the provision is meeting quality and productivity standards for the organization.

# Phase One

LPC's vision is "to be recognized as a critical business partner in achieving Lucent's success"; its mission is "to provide innovative learning solutions, readily available and highly valued worldwide, that measurably improve Lucent's organizational and individual performance."

Bill Harrod, LPC vice president, noted that many large organizations have an education committee, but such committees generally do not include people who are well informed about business needs. At Lucent, the education and training activities are divided into fifteen curriculum areas. Examples of curriculum areas include software, wireless, diversity, and program management. Each curriculum area has a business performance council, composed of powerful people in the company. For example, the software committee is headed by the vice president for software. There are more than 160 people on these councils. There is a dean for each curriculum, and about twenty subject matter experts help with curriculum design.

The business performance councils are responsible for much more than education and training. They consider all strategic issues related to the particular area. The point is that they specifically consider education and training as part of key strategic business issues. The success of the business performance councils and of the learning and development activities in general is driven by several factors including strong executive-level leadership and support and broad involvement with the business units.

The goal of the LPC unit is to be a valuable member of a team whose focus is much larger than learning. However, the learning staff must earn their way to the top management table by demonstrating how learning affects key business performance. The key is to understand the proficiency gaps in given business domains, determine which can be addressed by learning solutions, and develop learning solutions to help close those gaps.

The different business performance councils are at different stages in the development of tools for identifying competency gaps. A state-of-the-art tool, the Kiviat, is used by the software council. This tool helps assess proficiencies and identify gaps in eight software project areas: customer focus, project management, project team variables, tools, quality focus, methodologies, physical environment, and metrics. The tool includes a detailed instrument for measuring Lucent's performance (there are about 20 metrics in each area) on a five-point scale ranging from 1 (leading edge) to 5 (high risk). The performance measures are evaluated on the basis of ten years of industrywide data. The tool points out areas where Lucent's performance is not leading-edge; these are areas where learning might be able to improve business performance.

Harrod emphasized that just dumping courses out there will not solve the company's problems. There is a tendency to view all performance problems as "training problems"; however, not all proficiency gaps are due to a lack of skill or training. Individual jobs must be structured in such a way that employees can use the training they receive. A new initiative of the LPC is a consulting effort that works with the business units to identify the problems that are learning-related and design learning solutions for them. Rather than being an advocate for any and all education and training activities, the role of LPC is to help the company determine the most effective way to deploy limited education and training resources in such a way as to promote overall corporate goals. Part of that role is identifying where training is *not* appropriate. LPC recently established a consulting service that is specifically designed to work with the individual business units to help them find learning solutions when they are appropriate.

Another element of the LPC role is helping the company identify which stakeholder needs deserve attention from the learning and development unit. The purpose of learning activities at Lucent is to help the company achieve growth in key markets. If an activity is not important to Lucent from a business perspective, Lucent will not train it. LPC focuses on what people need to succeed on the job. Its activities focus on business needs, as distinct from student demands. Harrod noted that if Lucent were to offer a course on taxes on April 14th, a lot of employees would take the course. Employees would like it, but it is not relevant to business goals. In other words, there are "nice to have" courses and "need to have" courses. Lucent wants to focus on the "need to have."

As previously mentioned, an important part of LPC's early efforts were focused on eliminating redundancy and reducing cost. Much of this was achieved by consolidating approximately 70,000 courses taught throughout

Lucent into about 2,000. For example, there were originally about 700 courses on fire extinguisher operation. It has also decreased the number of vendors from which it purchases course content and eliminated certain high-cost programs whose value did not justify continuation (such as the Wharton executive MBA). LPC has also improved its focus on the courses it develops internally, having reduced that number from 800 to 390. Additionally, technology-enabled courses have reduced some travel costs. The total number of learner days has increased by over 60 percent.

The consolidation of courses has made it easier for Lucent to integrate training records with personnel records. Formerly, Lucent kept employee training records, but the records were not centralized. This made it difficult to construct a training history on an individual. Now, if a learner successfully completes a course, then course completion is recorded in the person's record. Lucent was using PeopleSoft for that purpose but has recently moved to a training server to track all training. In addition, the system allows workers to search for and enroll in courses online.

# Phase Two

The LPC provides some, but not all, of the education and professional development opportunities. The term "provider" is used loosely in this context and often refers to a situation where the LPC makes available to the business units a learning opportunity that was developed by an external provider. As a result, the LPC tends to operate as more of an intermediary (between the business units and the array of providers) than a provider, and Phase Two assessment is most similar to Model One.

### Identify Goals for Education and Training
The Lucent LPC has four layers of internal clients, ascribing different goals to learning activities. The executive leadership of Lucent wants LPC to promote cultural change (make Lucent look less like AT&T and more like a dot-com). Leaders at the vice president level want learning to promote strategic knowledge in the corporation. Mid-level managers are looking for tactical knowledge, and employees in general want the knowledge necessary to strengthen their roles in the company.

The goals of the learning activities are driven by input from business line leaders through the business performance councils. These councils have staff associated with the chief technical officer as well as the chief education officer. Because the same group of people is considering the technical and the training issues, the learning goals are driven by business needs.

Ultimately, the purpose of learning is to change an employee's behavior. Whereas education used to be just learner focused, now it is business focused.

### Develop Measures of Quality and Productivity

The main productivity measure used in LPC is cost per learner day (measured as eight hours spent in a learning activity). The LPC finds it is better to use the learner day rather than a course as the unit of analysis, because "courses" vary tremendously in their duration. The LPC would like to break the learning unit down further. Another metric it tracks is the percentage of programs that are technology enabled.

In terms of quality measurement, Lucent has made the most progress in two domains: software and program management. These are areas where there are externally based standards of knowledge and performance. In the area of program management, the Program Management Institute certifies program management skills and accredits courses designed to prepare learners for the tests.

Lucent uses the Kirkpatrick framework to develop measures of quality for education and development. It measures performance at levels 1, 2, and 3 and views level 1 as extremely important. Level 1 performance measures go beyond making training fun (or serving good food) so that the student provides positive course evaluations. The ultimate goal of a learning activity is to change the behavior of workers. If learners are not getting something they think they need, then they will not learn.

Level 2 is conducted for all learning experiences. Students must pass a test of some sort, and then successful completion of a learning module is recorded in their records (nothing is recorded if they fail). Level 3 assessment is being used in 30 to 40 percent of the learning activities; these assessments rely primarily on judgments made by managers of learners. LPC has not been asked to do level 4 assessment. Harrod believes that it is not possible to measure only the effects of learning activities because job performance is influenced by so many variables. In the future, LPC expects to adopt a balanced scorecard approach to identify goals and develop measures.

### *Evaluate Quality and Productivity Using Measures*

LPC wants to see high learner satisfaction (level 1) results because it believes that this is a good measure of whether students found the coursework relevant to their jobs.

To the extent possible, LPC benchmarks itself against other learning organizations and strives to be at the leading edge of such organizations. It also compares current performance to previous performance. LPC has reduced the average cost per learner day from $520 to $284. The primary source of savings comes from the use of technology and courses developed in the marketplace. Currently, 20 percent of the learning is technology enabled. The goal is to reach 50 percent.

The learning network model suggests a continuous process of assessing competency gaps, feeding results to the business councils, and changing training to address the identified gaps and other needs. The whole point is that the results of learning activities and the assessment of those activities will influence the day-to-day operation of Lucent. Harrod emphasized the power of measurement to drive performance.

# Appendix B: Process Auditors—Academic Audit

THE ACADEMIC AUDIT is a relatively new approach to quality assessment that has been implemented abroad—in Hong Kong, Scandinavia, Great Britain, Australia, New Zealand, and the Association of European Universities (CRE)—and has begun to receive attention from U.S. accrediting organizations. The academic audit is an external peer review of institutional quality assessment and improvement systems at a particular provider institution. The focus of the audit is on an institution's own processes for measuring and improving academic quality.

The academic audit originated in 1990 in the United Kingdom when the government became increasingly interested in ensuring that sufficient attention was paid to teaching in the face of rapid growth in higher education. A threat existed that Her Majesty's Inspector (HMI) would undertake an audit of colleges and universities. Instead, the Academic Standards Group of the Committee of Vice Chancellors and Principals recommended the creation of an Academic Audit Unit (AAU) to provide external and independent assurance that U.K. universities had adequate and effective mechanisms and structures for monitoring, maintaining, and improving the quality of their teaching (Dill, 2000a, p. 189). Implementing the audit process precluded an evaluation from HMI.

The emergence of the academic audit is related in part to the changing global market for education, which is increasing pressure on higher education worldwide. Particularly in Europe, where higher education has traditionally been run by the state, the issue facing education policymakers is how to create markets. In the United States, market forces have been at work for many years. This market pressure has induced institutions to maintain or improve quality. Dill suggests that the academic audit caught on in other countries first because they are more seriously looking for something beyond market forces that can help with quality improvement.

Academic audits normally are conducted by an intermediary organization, not a customer or the provider. The team of auditors typically includes generalists, not subject experts, although audit teams usually include faculty members experienced in teaching and academic work. The exact size and composition of audit teams vary across countries. In Hong Kong, audits are carried out by the University Grants Committee, which is a nonstatutory advisory body whose members include distinguished overseas academics, prominent local professionals and businesspeople, and senior, locally based academics (see Massy and French, 1997). This committee includes local academics to "encourage mutual learning and acceptance of the process locally" (http://www.ugc.edu.hk/english/documents/papers/wfm_njfs.html). According to the perspective of outside evaluators, the academic audit appears to encourage collaboration among stakeholders, providers, and the intermediary.

An academic audit typically involves three steps: (1) the inspection of documents supplied by the university under review (self-assessment), (2) a visit by a team of auditors, and (3) the writing of a report (by the auditors). In Hong Kong, the institution prepares a twenty-page report describing its quality improvement and assurance measures. The review team assesses the documentation, visits the institution, and compiles a report. The steps in the U.K. audit are similar to those used in Hong Kong as well as to the process for accreditation in the United States: institutions submit materials to the review team, the review team conducts a site visit to the institution, and then the review team issues a report. After going through the materials sent by the provider, the audit team typically visits the institution for several days and interviews dozens of representatives, including senior administrators, quality assurance committee members, department and/or program heads, and students. The team's findings are then documented in a report that should focus on processes rather than individuals.

The unit of analysis for academic audits is usually whole institutions, but the assessment could work with individual programs or departments. In fact, the audit of an institution usually involves a review of a sample of programs. Because it is difficult to audit all departments at one time, Dill suggests sampling departments randomly rather than relying on volunteers, as volunteers will likely be an unrepresentative sample of the quality processes in an institution.

The objective of an academic audit is to ensure that institutions have processes in place for measuring their own quality and thus can engage in ongoing self-improvement. Each institution is treated on its own terms, and audit reports are written principally with the institution in mind. Auditors do not compare institutions. It is this self-assessment that ultimately leads to quality improvement. The audit process usually includes a publicly available report that serves as a form of accountability. Publicizing the report motivates the institution to take the process more seriously and enables the public to verify that institutions have processes in place to ensure quality. Further, in Hong Kong, using the report to inform funding decisions has been discussed.

The academic audit is related to total quality management (TQM), continuous quality improvement, the Baldrige Award, and the process-oriented tradition. These techniques are informed by the business literature. To the extent that the Baldrige Award, TQM, and other business-oriented quality processes have been used in higher education, they have been in the operating (and other nonacademic) departments. The academic audit has been more successful in permeating higher education because it is less adversarial and more "academic." Dill believes that academics have resisted a direct application of business techniques as foreign, hostile, and not in sync with the university culture. Academics view the academic audit as less alien because this process originated in the academic community and is based on a research orientation that builds evidence to support quality assertions.

According to Dill, academic audits are efficient forms of assessment relative to alternatives such as accreditation, subject review, and program review. Subject reviews are in depth and can result in a high level of accountability for a specific area. But they are also very costly. The cost/benefit ratio tends to be very low. Audits are much more efficient.

Identification and analysis of best practices can follow from an academic audit. Although the audits are general and open ended, experience shows that good departments employ certain types of quality assessment practices. For example, the quality assurance agency in the U.K. has generated two *Learning from Audit* reports on best practices. Best practices have also emerged from the Hong Kong and CRE efforts (Dill, 2000a). The CRE holds an annual conference for the institutions that were audited that year. This conference provides audited schools an opportunity to share what they learned from the experience and the best practices that emerged. Over time, such a review of best practices might help an intermediary develop minimum standards for an audit process.

Implementation of academic audit processes has generally been incremental and collegial, with substantial input from the schools themselves. Providers spent a lot of time looking at how other institutions implemented the academic audit. Some countries piloted the academic audit process to obtain gradual buy-in. In the U.K., and to some extent in Scandinavia and Australia, formal training is available for those who conduct academic audits. Audit manuals and audit visit protocols are also available from some of these countries. Organizations interested in the academic audit typically visit and learn from the organizations that have already implemented it. The audit teams in Hong Kong, for example, included experts from other countries. Although organizations do learn from one another, they tend not to implement the academic audit exactly as another organization or country has done. Rather, they mold it to fit their own circumstances.

The academic audit assumes that good people working with sufficient resources and following good processes will produce good results, while deficient processes will make it difficult for even good people with ample resources to produce optimal outcomes. In addition, the audit assumes that quality processes can be identified and articulated through self-study and verified by an outside team through interviews with faculty and staff.

Dill points out that the academic audit may be a transitional process that will fizzle out as market-generated assessment tools (e.g., *U.S. News & World Report,* industry certifications) become more prominent overseas. A question exists about the long-term viability of the academic audit. Thus far, the countries that have completed one audit cycle have found it to be useful, have modified it, and are signing on for another cycle. Whether this process will continue is unclear.

# Phase One

Academic audits are designed for use with individual provider institutions. The intermediaries who conduct the audits are not, therefore, interested in assessing the needs of the larger system, although they may insert system-level goals into the audit process. Phase One activities are therefore not relevant to the academic audit process.

# Phase Two

The academic audit is an example of Model One. In an academic audit, the provider institution assesses itself, and an intermediary evaluates the self-assessment. The intermediary may prescribe the process and may dictate a limited number of goals, but the provider, for the most part, is in control of its own assessment. The intermediary then certifies the assessment process.

### Identify Goals for Education and Training

As mentioned, the premise behind the academic audit is that the intermediary (auditing organization) assesses the provider institution's internal quality process. Although the auditor may establish certain parameters for acceptable goals, the institutions are generally responsible for setting their own goals for the education activities in which they are engaged. According to Dill, goals for the audit process were unclear when audits were first implemented but are becoming clearer over time. In other words, as institutions become familiar with the audit process, they tend to focus on similar goals. Currently, three common goals are typically used as a base for an academic audit. "Auditors review and verify the effectiveness of an institution's basic processes of academic quality assurance and improvement by: 1) how an institution designs, monitors, and evaluates academic programs and degrees; 2) how an institution assesses, evaluates, and improves teaching and student learning; and 3) how an institution takes account of the views of external stakeholders in improving teaching and student learning" (Dill, 2000b). Additional goals should reflect the individual culture and mission of the institution being reviewed.

In the U.K., auditors determine whether institutions have processes in place for assuring quality in relation to mission, institutional policies, strategies and operational procedures, institutional resources and organization, staff and student recruitment and development, institutional leadership, research, design of courses and degree programs, teaching methods, involvement of stakeholders, teacher evaluation, and assessing learning outcomes. The academic audit visit itself consists of an extensive investigation of three to four processes that the audit team selects based on what was submitted by the institution.

## Develop Measures of Quality and Productivity

The academic audit delegates the selection and development of measures to the provider. The auditing agency may submit broad guidelines to the institution to help it select performance measures, but it generally gives institutions flexibility over the data they submit. Massy and French (1999) caution against system-level performance measures, noting that "'one size fits all' performance measures should be viewed with suspicion." They believe that in an academic audit, performance measures should be developed at the program or institutional level.

Because it emphasizes process, the academic audit has been criticized for a lack of attention to inputs and outcomes. The academic audit, however, does not so much ignore outcomes as delegate responsibility for assessing outcomes to the provider. In fact, Dill stressed that audits are increasingly focusing on outcome measures, pressing the institutions to examine their measures and how they know that the measures are reliable and valid indicators of what they are trying to accomplish.

In the U.K., the AAU suggests materials that institutions might submit as part of the academic audit, including formal publications (such as annual reports), codes of practice, official policies, internal handbooks, external examiner reports, new course approval documents, and meeting minutes. Other supporting documentation may include mechanisms for monitoring academic quality and means of providing support for academic quality improvement.

### *Evaluate Quality and Productivity Using Measures*

Intermediaries typically do not prescribe a specific template or model against which quality processes will be measured. Each institution is treated on its own terms, and audit reports are written principally with the institution in mind. Results are not compared with other institutions' academic audits. Neither are there set standards against which to compare results. The academic audit, therefore, is sensitive to the different roles, missions, and characteristics of institutions. As a result, it is particularly useful for systems with a diverse set of providers.

# Appendix C: State Higher Education Boards

STATE HIGHER EDUCATION BOARDS work under the authority of the governor and legislature, with the purpose of ensuring a constructive relationship between postsecondary institutions and the state. Boards vary in their responsibilities, influence, and level of authority over higher education institutions. Three examples of state boards include consolidated governing boards, coordinating boards, and planning boards. Governing boards, as implied by their name, govern individual higher education institutions through planning, problem resolution, program review, budget and policy development, personnel appointment, and resource allocation. Coordinating boards do not govern individual institutions. They instead tend to focus on planning for the statewide system as a whole. These boards may review and even approve both budget requests and academic programs. They do not, however, appoint personnel or develop policies for individual institutions. Planning boards are typically voluntary rather than statutory. These boards facilitate communications between individual institutions and states but do no governing or coordinating activities.

In response to mandates from state legislators or governors, most boards have created "accountability systems," or structured efforts to measure and ensure the quality of the institutions within their purview. Among the accountability systems in vogue today are performance indicators, report cards, and performance funding. Although accountability is the primary purpose of these systems, most states encourage institutions to use the data for self-improvement as well.

Accountability systems differ in the level of collaboration among stakeholders, providers, and intermediaries. Some higher education boards are more directive than others. When governing boards determine assessment goals, measures, and evaluations without substantial input from providers, conflict and resentment often follow. Institutional leaders may feel that the state is imposing on them standards that do not reflect the institution's actual quality. Other state boards are more collaborative and ask institutions to play a substantial role in establishing assessment goals and methods. Although this approach leads to more acceptance of assessment by providers, it is time-consuming and costly.

The information gathered through these accountability systems is used in at least four ways, including:

- **Funding.** Some states link a percentage of funding to institutional performance. Tennessee awards 2 to 5 percent of its instructional budget based on assessment results. In theory, South Carolina awards 100 percent of funding based on performance, but in practice a much smaller percentage (probably about 5 percent) depends on assessment results (Schmidt, 1999).
- **Program Planning and Elimination.** Assessment results may contribute to decision-making about academic programs. For example, based on its review of assessment data, the Illinois Boards of Higher Education in 1992 recommended the elimination, consolidation, or reduction of 190 programs at public universities, including 7 percent of all undergraduate programs, among other changes.
- **Comparisons.** In many states individual campuses are encouraged to use assessment results for self-improvement purposes. The degree to which this actually occurs is unknown.
- **Public Information.** Assessment results also provide a means of informing the public about their state's higher education system. Thus, some states publish report cards—for the system as a whole or for individual institutions.

The effectiveness of state accountability systems is uneven. At best, the efforts may lead to quality improvements and better alignment between higher education and state policy goals. At worst, the efforts create dissension, force institutions to redirect resources away from other arguably more valuable activities, and provide little insight into the performance of higher education institutions and systems.

## Phase One

Most state boards are involved in coordinating their statewide systems of higher education. Such coordination ensures that postsecondary institutions operate collectively in ways that are aligned with state priorities and that serve the public interest (McGuinness, 1997). Coordinating efforts can be achieved through both long-range or master planning and focused research studies. A detailed example of Phase One assessment at the state level will be provided in Appendix C1.

## Phase Two

State-level accountability and assessment systems most resemble Model Two. Whether conducted under the guise of performance indicators, performance funding, or report card programs, state boards choose the goals upon which the assessment is to be based and then collect information from institutions and make judgments on this information. However, there are states that tend to use a version of Model One. Appendix C2 describes how the Kentucky board allows higher education institutions to determine their own "fitness for purpose" upon which assessments are based. In addition, some other states use a version of Model Four. Florida, for example, has a statewide rising junior exam for college students at the sophomore level. Legislation passed in 1995 limited the use of this exam, called the "College Level Academic Skills Test" (CLAST), so that students can bypass the test if they score well on the Scholastic Aptitude Test (SAT) or if they perform well in specific courses. Nonetheless, use of the CLAST is an example of Model Four assessment. Even Model Three may be relevant to some state boards. While Model Three involves a higher education institution conducting its own assessment, state boards can provide information to help institutions assess themselves or incentive funding to induce institutions to conduct specific assessments. Uses of Model Three were in vogue in many states in the early 1980s (Ewell, 1999a).

**Identify Goals for Education and Training.** State accountability systems focus on goals linked to the state's overall higher education mission (reflecting the needs of the general public and corporate, civic, and political leaders), rather than individual institutions' missions. Typically, the goals address such issues as educational access and affordability, quality and effectiveness, diversity and equity, efficiency and productivity, contribution to state needs, and connection to other education sectors (e.g., K–12). Goals may relate to inputs, processes, outputs, and outcomes. Goals may be established by the state legislature, governor, or the coordinating/governing board.

**Develop Measures of Quality and Productivity.** In some cases, states mandate measures with little input from the institutions. In other states, the selection of measures is the result of extended discussion and negotiation between institutions and governing/coordinating boards. The measures that constitute state accountability systems vary on several dimensions.

- **The number of measures.** Although institutions generally want more measures included in an assessment program—to maximize the likelihood of high performance on at least some measures—this approach also increases costs. Thus, the costs of assessment are less in Tennessee, with its 15 measures, than in South Carolina, with 37.
- **The level of control exercised by the state.** Some states, such as Colorado, encourage institutions to select measures that satisfy internal institutional improvement needs. Others, such as South Carolina, prescribe the measures. Most states are plagued by ambiguity in operational definitions and measurement methodology. For example, student-faculty ratios can be calculated in different ways, leading to significantly different results.
- **The unit of analysis.** Whole institutions are the typical unit of analysis for accountability systems. Within this unit of analysis, politicians seem to be most interested in student-related variables, such as institutional retention rates and pass rates on licensing examinations.
- **Data sources.** In most cases, measures are culled from major institutional databases, from such areas as admissions, registration, and finance. Other measures are based on unit-level data, such as library-use statistics. Still

others, such as satisfaction surveys, require new data collection, often at substantial cost. Some states, such as Texas and Virginia, have developed large centralized databases that provide the state board direct access to a wide range of data for assessment. Most, however, rely on institutions to report the results of requested analyses.

- **Measurement focus.** Since the 1980s, accountability systems have tended to emphasize outcomes. Scholars are stressing, however, that assessment systems should place equal emphasis on the processes that lead to outcomes, so decisionmakers will understand what changes they need to make to have an effect on outcomes (Banta and Borden, 1994).
- **Measurement variation.** Some states apply the same measures to a wide range of institutional types. Other states use different measures for different types of institutions.

Typical accountability measures, or indicators, address admission standards, characteristics of incoming students, admissions "yield" rates, enrollment, total student credit hours, transfer rates, retention and graduation rates, student time to degree, degrees awarded, professional licensure exam pass rates, results of satisfaction surveys (by students, alumni, and employers), faculty teaching workload, and extramural or sponsored research funds.

Tennessee's accountability system, now more than twenty years old, was developed in response to the implementation of performance-based funding in the 1970s. The accountability system has undergone a number of changes—most recently, the state started issuing report cards for each institution. Table C1 displays the indicators used in the report card.

South Carolina has also developed a strong accountability system, the major elements of which are displayed in Table C2.

**Evaluate Quality and Productivity Using Measures.** Generally, the coordinating or governing board carries out an evaluation process using data submitted by institutions. Institutional performance may be compared to state-set standards (e.g., South Carolina), peer group performance, or past performance (e.g., Tennessee).

**TABLE C1**
**Report Card Indicators Used in Tennessee**

| Categories | Indicators |
|---|---|
| Student learning | Licensure examination pass-rates |
| | Job placement (percentage) |
| | Student satisfaction (satisfaction survey responses) |
| | Alumni satisfaction (survey responses) |
| | Core knowledge and skills (performance on national tests) |
| | Graduation rates |
| | Degree granted |
| Academic programs | Program accreditation (percentage eligible accredited) |
| | External peer review (number meeting standards) |
| Faculty productivity | Hours of instruction |
| | Students per class |
| Financial accountability | Tuition and fees |
| | Staffing (number full-time) |
| | Expenditures (by function) |
| | Private giving |
| | Financial aid (percentage of students receiving aid) |

## TABLE C2
## Performance Measures Used in South Carolina

| Categories | Indicators |
|---|---|
| Mission focus | Expenditures to achieve mission |
| | Curricula offered to achieve mission |
| | Approval of a mission statement |
| | Adoption of strategic plan |
| | Attainment of strategic plan goals |
| Quality of faculty | Academic and other faculty credentials |
| | Performance review (to include student and peer evaluation) |
| | Posttenure review |
| | Compensation |
| | Faculty availability to students outside class |
| | Community and public service |
| Instructional quality | Class size and student-teacher ratio |
| | Number of credit hours taught by faculty |
| | Ratio of full-time faculty as compared with other full-time employees |
| | Accreditation of degree-granting programs |
| | Institutional emphasis on teacher education quality and reform |
| Institutional cooperation and collaboration | Sharing and use of technology and other resources internally and with external partners |
| | Collaboration with private industry |
| Administrative efficiency | Administrative and academic cost comparisons |
| | Use of best management practices |
| | Elimination of waste and duplication |
| | General overhead costs per FTE student |
| Entrance requirements | SAT and ACT scores of student body |
| | High school standing, GPA, and student activities |
| | Nonacademic achievements of students |
| | In-state student enrollment |

*(Continued)*

## TABLE C2
## Performance Measures Used in South Carolina   (*Continued*)

| *Categories* | *Indicators* |
|---|---|
| Graduates' achievements | Graduation rate |
| | Employment rate for graduates |
| | Employer feedback on graduates |
| | Scores on professional exams |
| | Graduates continuing education in state |
| | Credit hours earned of graduates |
| User-friendliness of institution | Credit transfer to and from institution |
| | Continuing education units |
| | Accessibility of institution to state citizens |
| Research funding | Grants for teacher education |
| | Public and private sector grants |

*Notes:* FTE is full-time equivalent. ACT is American College Testing. GPA is grade point average.

# Appendix C1: Texas Higher Education Coordinating Board

T HE TEXAS HIGHER EDUCATION COORDINATING BOARD was established in 1965 by the state legislature. Its overall objective is to promote quality and efficiency in the higher education system. The coordinating board serves as an intermediary between the state legislature and the institutions, and its responsibilities fall into three major areas:

- **Coordination:** The coordinating board works with the legislature, governor, and institutional governing boards to coordinate Texas higher education to expand access, improve quality, and promote efficiency through such actions as developing higher education plans, reviewing and approving degree programs, and constructing of major facilities.
- **Information:** The coordinating board provides information on higher education to state policymakers and citizens.
- **Administration:** The coordinating board administers state and federal programs.

The Texas system consists of 120 public and private institutions—three-quarters are four-year, and one-quarter are technical or community colleges. Fifty-four percent of students are enrolled in the four-year institutions, and 46 percent are enrolled in community or technical colleges. There are 966,840 students in all of postsecondary higher education in Texas. The state expects enrollment in public institutions to continue increasing over the next five years.

In terms of assessing higher education's quality and productivity, the coordinating board's main tool is its authority to approve and/or close programs—more specifically, approve the programs for state funding according to an established formula. The coordinating board conducts two types of reviews at the program level:

1. Initial reviews of programs that institutions would like to offer. Approval by the board is required for the program to be eligible for state funding.
2. Ongoing reviews of programs that have been approved by the board.

Programs must be approved by the board to be eligible for state funding. Programs can lose their approval in the ongoing review, although that rarely happens. Coordinating board staff members know that they will approve some programs that are not worthwhile (about 10 percent will be bad investments); it is impossible to avoid such mistakes. It is important, however, to constantly reevaluate the need for existing programs so as to minimize the effects of mistakes.

In addition to approving and reviewing programs, the board evaluates the effectiveness of the community and technical colleges in the state. The "institutional effectiveness process" is a "comprehensive approach for verifying the effectiveness of Texas' community and technical colleges in achieving their local and statutory missions" (p.1). Extensive information is gathered from community colleges to evaluate their effectiveness. These data are maintained in a longitudinal database that allows for a strong tracking capability. Every fall, the coordinating board creates an incoming cohort and tracks them as a group for seven years. Students can be tracked across colleges or systems, or even into the workforce by linking Social Security numbers to Texas workforce commission data. As a result, institutions know where their graduates go and can answer such questions as: Do community college graduates go on to a four-year college? If so, do they eventually graduate? Do graduates get jobs in the state of Texas?

Although these data are collected annually, overall institutional effectiveness is measured through a peer-review process with a site visit every four years. This site visit accomplishes both the institutional effectiveness review and the individual program-level review.

The purpose of initial program review and ongoing reviews is both accountability (ensuring that the institutions are spending state money for useful purposes) and program improvement. Similarly, the purpose of the institutional effectiveness process is to hold the community and technical colleges accountable to meeting their missions and to help them improve. The assessment processes are intended to benefit various stakeholders, including legislators, the public, and students, and to assist the institutions in their quests for improvement.

All of these assessment efforts are controlled by the coordinating board, acting as an intermediary. The initial program review includes a market assessment that encourages collaboration between providers and stakeholders. Ongoing reviews at the community and technical colleges also involve an advisory board that includes people from outside the institution, suggesting that stakeholder involvement is promoted during this process.

Initially, colleges were resistant to the coordinating board's role as the main information resource. Resistance diminished as the institutions came to see value in the published reports and online data. In the past, many colleges did not have the capability to provide the data required by the Southern Association of Colleges and Schools and did not have the resources to manipulate any existing data. Currently, the coordinating board not only analyzes the data it receives from institutions, but it packages the information for redistribution to colleges and other interested organizations. Due partly to these efforts, the colleges' response to the coordinating board's assessment efforts has been very positive.

## Phase One

The coordinating board engages in statewide higher education planning processes. One of these planning efforts involved developing the Workforce Education Course Manual, which is "the state community and technical college inventory of workforce education courses" (see http://www.thecb.state.tx.us/ctc/ip/wecm2000/main.htm). Developing this manual was a substantial and ambitious effort. To develop the manual, the coordinating board gathered experts and faculty together and got them to agree on a set of courses, an appropriate content description, and a range of "contact" hours for courses in particular sequences. This process was in response to excessive program

---

duplication and insufficient transferability of courses from one institution to another. The manual is an attempt at eliminating both of these roadblocks. During this manual development process, course duplications were uncovered and remedied. For example, the number of welding courses was reduced from 900 to 96. Now, every college that offers introductory welding calls it the same name (e.g., Welding 101). The course involves the same number of contact hours regardless of where it is delivered. Now, a person can take Welding 101 in Del Rio, and then be ready to take Welding 102 in San Antonio. Overall, the number of courses offered throughout the state by the community and technical colleges went from more than 30,000 to approximately 6,000.

This manual has had two effects: (1) businesses know that programs are the same in each college, and (2) students can transfer credits from one institution to another without difficulty. The Workforce Education Course Manual effort took approximately four years and cost approximately $150,000 per year.

# Phase Two

The assessment process used in Texas most closely resembles Model Two. The intermediary decides the criteria upon which the assessments are conducted. This intermediary (the coordinating board) then collects data and judges whether the program under review is worthy of either initial or continued funding.

### *Identify Goals for Education and Training*

Underlying goals are evident in the initial program approval process. This process is based on five criteria. The criteria are not literally goals but guiding principles for evaluation. The coordinating board has used the following criteria since its inception:

1. Need: Does the state need this program at this institution?
2. Quality: Are new programs of good quality (thus protecting student interests)?
3. Cost: Is the program worth the cost?
4. Duplication: Does the program duplicate existing programs?
5. Mission: Does the program fall within the scope of the institution's mission?

In addition to these five criteria for program approval, there are seven standards of program and institutional quality that must be adhered to by the community and technical colleges. Institutions must

- Fulfill their statutory mandate and meet the unique needs of their service area
- Use Perkins resources effectively (as mandated by the federal Perkins Act)
- Provide sufficient access and effective student services
- Ensure student achievement
- Provide quality continuing education
- Provide quality academic programs and services
- Provide quality workforce education programs.

### Develop Measures of Quality and Productivity

The measures of quality and productivity differ for initial program approvals, ongoing reviews at universities, and ongoing reviews at two-year colleges. In general, the initial program approval process uses similar measures at universities and two-year colleges.

**Initial Program Approval.** Measures are categorized according to the goals to which they relate:

1. The need criterion looks at student and job demand. Does the state need this program at this institution? Different types of data collection methods are used to answer this question, including surveys, national data on doctoral programs, occupational handbooks for job demand projections in particular sectors, the link to the Texas economy, and the relative number of programs in Texas with respect to other states in the country. At the technical and community college level, the program under consideration must have a business advisory board.

2. The quality criterion is based on the rationale of protecting students' interests. The quality indicator focuses on faculty and resources (i.e., whether engineering programs have adequate labs and facilities). It also considers things such as whether there are enough faculty members to staff the program. For example, there is an informal standard of a minimum of four

FTE faculty members for doctoral programs. One coordinating board member said, "We want planned programs that have a national reputation." In addition, the quality assessment considers Southern Association of Colleges and Schools accreditation and qualification of faculty.

At community and technical colleges, the coordinating board also looks at whether the institution has started any relevant external accreditation process where such a quality assessment process is available (e.g., programs for dental assistants). The coordinating board also looks at how the college is doing in other programs. If the college is not meeting standards in other areas, it may be prevented from starting a new program.

3. The cost criterion examines the projected cost to the state. The state wants to know whether or not programs will be self-supporting after they have been initiated. Programs with high cost and low funding or demand do not make sense. The coordinating board asks for detailed accounts of how the proposed program will be funded during the start-up phase. Since enrollment-based funding is based on enrollment from previous years, a new program will not generate revenues in real time.

4. The duplication criterion looks at whether higher education institutions within a given geographic area have similar programs.

5. The mission criterion simply looks at whether the program falls within an institution's mission.

**Ongoing Program Review—Universities.** In reviewing existing programs at universities, the coordinating board relies to a large extent on accreditation; programs should meet Southern Association of Colleges and Schools and program-specific accrediting agency standards. Other than this measure, the coordinating board does not systematically examine the quality of programs, except in the area of teacher education. The legislature has been focused on teacher education and is concerned about the quality of graduates from teacher education programs. The coordinating board has imposed additional requirements on teacher education programs, including more interdisciplinary studies, a larger number of required math courses, and the elimination of math and science courses designed just for students in the education programs. In other words, the board is directly intervening in the process by instituting specific curricular requirements. The board also collects and reports information on the pass rates of licensing exams for graduates of professional programs.

In addition to examining ongoing program quality at the four-year institutions, the coordinating board is involved in ongoing productivity reviews. Publications are available on classroom utilization, research expenditures, and research funding per faculty member. In addition, programs must graduate at least three Ph.D.s within a five-year period to be considered productive.

**Ongoing Review—Two-Year Colleges.** The coordinating board's measurement of performance of two-year colleges is more involved than it is for the universities. This review is conducted through an on-site peer review process. Conducted every four years, this process not only serves as a program review process, but also as a method for evaluating institutional effectiveness. Therefore, the coordinating board asks for data on both program-level assessment and the meeting of the seven statewide goals mentioned previously. A committee of college presidents, faculty, students, and industry representatives identified 66 different measures to be collected from each two-year institution to meet these seven goals. The state legislature's budget board passed a law requiring all two-year colleges in the state to collect these data. Table C3 displays some examples of the measures the coordinating board uses to determine whether these goals have been achieved.

This table is not an exhaustive list; each goal typically has five to ten measures. For the most part, information is provided by the institutions, but some information is available from external sources. Approximately $530,000 is used to support this data collection effort annually.

### Evaluate Quality and Productivity Using Measures

In approving new programs, the coordinating board compares institutional data on the new program with the existing five criteria. In reviewing existing programs, the process is much more involved for the community and technical colleges. For the four-year institutions, the coordinating board basically ensures that the program is accredited, although it does examine the teacher preparation programs in greater detail. These examinations are, again, made in reference to existing standards. For the community and technical colleges, institutional data are again compared with existing standards. However, the

## TABLE C3
## Examples of Measures for Texas Two-Year Colleges

| Goals | Examples of Measures |
|---|---|
| Fulfill their statutory mandate and meet the unique needs of their service area | Published mission statement addresses all statutory requirements |
| Use Perkins resources effectively | Current funds must be expended on allowable costs |
| Provide sufficient access and effective student services | Proportion of women and minorities in all workforce education enrollment is comparable (within 5 percent) to overall college enrollment or shows improvement compared with overall college enrollment |
| Ensure student achievement | 30 percent of full-time, first-time-in-college students not receiving remediation receive a degree or certificate or transfer within three years |
| Provide quality continuing education | College shows documented evidence of serving literacy needs in the college district (either through college efforts or collaboration with other entities) offering certain programs* |
| Provide quality academic programs and services | The college has incorporated a core curriculum of at least 42 semester credit hours into each academic degree plan, unless a smaller core curriculum component is specified in a statewide field of study curriculum |
| Provide quality workforce education programs | Program must have had 15 graduates over last three years |

*Adult basic education, general equivalency diploma, English-as-second-language, and Workforce Literary programs.

board's general philosophy is to allow colleges to draw their own conclusions and make their own decisions based on the reports provided. So colleges use reports to facilitate decision-making, while the coordinating board plays a supportive role and assists the colleges where needed.

# Appendix C2: Kentucky Council on Postsecondary Education

THE KENTUCKY SYSTEM of higher education consists of two research universities (The University of Louisville and The University of Kentucky), The Kentucky Commonwealth Virtual University, six comprehensive regional universities, and a system of 28 community and technical colleges. These institutions serve approximately 47,000 credit and 144,000 noncredit students each year.

The Kentucky governor has made higher education a defining issue of his administration. In 1996, the Kentucky General Assembly adopted Senate Concurrent Resolution 93, which created the Task Force on Postsecondary Education. This task force commissioned a review of postsecondary education in Kentucky and published the results in March 1997. This report spurred further legislation, which established five goals for the state to achieve by 2020, called *2020 Vision: An Agenda for Kentucky's System of Postsecondary Education.*

This same legislation mandated the mission for the Kentucky Council on Postsecondary Education (CPE), which is Kentucky's coordinating board for their higher education system.[15] The purpose of the CPE, an intermediary in this system,[16] is to provide factual information to state political leaders, to adopt a statewide agenda that provides direction to the system, and to eliminate duplication and wasteful competition. The CPE is charged with leading the reform efforts envisioned by state policy leaders. Council members have pledged reduced bureaucracy, staunch advocacy, decisive management, and effective stewardship to achieve six results:

- Public support for the value of postsecondary education.

- Information that is helpful to students and their families in making educational decisions.
- An educational system that is well coordinated and efficient.
- Incentives that stimulate change and prompt institutions to redesign programs and services, realign resources for priorities to improve productivity, and generate new resources.
- Information that shows the public how the system and its institutions are performing.
- Data and research that help policymakers make good decisions.

CPE has 50 employees—half support and half professional. Under guidance of its mission, the CPE's work involves coordinating the improvement of Kentucky postsecondary education. Some of what CPE does is regulatory (approval of new academic programs, for instance), and some is advisory (such as budget recommendations to the governor and the general assembly). State legislation also gave CPE control over the allocation of incentive funds. In addition, CPE licenses the private institutions in the state. Finally, CPE was specifically assigned with developing and implementing a strategic agenda, as well as performance indicators to track the progress of the five goals listed in *2020 Vision,* which is the mechanism the state uses to assess its higher education system.

This assessment process is intended to promote improvement within institutions and the system as a whole and to hold institutions accountable to the state and its citizens. The assessment is stakeholder-driven, because it is motivated and guided by the governor and the legislature. The assessment process is designed to benefit all stakeholders, including legislators, the governor, students, graduates, business owners, and all citizens. The assessment process is an important tool that lets the governor and the legislature monitor the progress of individual institutions and the higher education system as a whole.

Each year, CPE produces a status report for the governor and the legislature discussing progress toward the *2020 Vision* goals. Information from the assessment process, including comparisons to national standards, influences funding.

# Phase One

Creating the Task Force on Postsecondary Education in 1996 was a first step in Phase One assessment in the state of Kentucky. Task force members completed a basic needs analysis of higher education throughout the state. They found low participation in postsecondary education and below-average per-capita income that was, in their opinion, creating a vicious cycle. The task force concluded that postsecondary education was the key to prosperity—for their citizens, their businesses, their communities, and their children. Therefore, in the broadest sense, the mission of the Kentucky system of postsecondary education became economic development. The task force concluded that a responsive and flexible system of postsecondary education needed to become a key tool in helping Kentucky flourish in the early decades of the 21st century. Greater economic prosperity could be achieved by making it possible for all Kentuckians to participate in lifelong learning. These Phase One activities culminated in *2020 Vision,* the goals for higher education in the state.

Phase One activities continue through the Strategic Committee on Postsecondary Education, which brings together state policy leaders in a forum to exchange ideas about the future of postsecondary education in Kentucky. Its members (including the governor, legislative leaders, the CPE members and president, and other representatives) play a pivotal role in assuring that the efforts of the postsecondary education system have the long-term support of policymakers and are tied to statewide needs and economic well-being.

# Phase Two

The assessment process used in Kentucky most closely resembles Model Two. The legislature has defined the goals, and an intermediary collects information on whether the individual institutions are meeting the goals by gathering data from the institutions. However, measures for whether the institutions are meeting the goals were developed through extensive collaboration with diverse stakeholders. The intermediary then determines the extent to which each institution has met the state's goals.

### *Identify Goals for Education and Training*

The five goals for the assessment process were delineated in the 1997 legislation that created *2020 Vision*. The intent is to achieve these goals by the year 2020. The following text is from *2020 Vision*:

> *We ask you to envision a Kentucky in the year 2020 recognized throughout the nation and across the world for having:*

- Educated citizens who want advanced knowledge and skills and know how to acquire them; and who are good parents, good citizens, and economically self-sufficient workers.
- Globally competitive businesses and industries respected for their highly knowledgeable employees and the technological sophistication of their products and services.
- Vibrant communities offering a standard of living unsurpassed by those in other states and nations.
- Scholars and practitioners who are among the best in the world, dedicated to creating new ideas, technologies, and knowledge.
- An integrated system of elementary and secondary schools and providers of postsecondary education, committed to meeting the needs of students and the Commonwealth, and acclaimed for excellence, innovation, collaboration, and responsiveness.

The primary purpose of these goals is to bring Kentucky up to the national average in terms of quality-of-life indicators. While these goals' scope goes beyond the traditional scope of higher education institutions, these institutions will play specific roles to move the state toward achieving the goals. The Kentucky Community and Technical College System will be the primary provider of two-year transfer and technical programs, workforce training for existing and new businesses and industries, and remedial and continuing education to improve the quality of life and employability of the citizens of the Commonwealth. The regional universities (Eastern Kentucky University, Kentucky State University, Morehead State University, Murray State University, Northern Kentucky University, and Western Kentucky University) will work cooperatively to ensure statewide access to appropriate, high-quality baccalaureate and master's degree programs. Each university will develop at least one program of national distinction. The University of Louisville will be a premier, nationally recognized metropolitan research university. The University of Kentucky will be a major comprehensive research institution ranked nationally among the top 20 public universities.

In addition to these specific roles, CPE needs to identify goals for educational quality that incorporate the views of all stakeholders. Because of the challenges involved in understanding the views of certain stakeholders, CPE has hired a consulting company to conduct focus groups with students, alumni, parents, and employers to determine what they think a "quality education" entails.

### *Develop Measures of Quality and Productivity*

CPE, in conjunction with individual college leaders, wrote an action agenda that addresses how it will implement *2020 Vision* goals over the next four years. In writing this agenda, CPE also got feedback from a range of Kentuckians through teleconferences, radio shows, meetings, telephone interviews, and focus groups. These activities targeted involvement of campus administrators, faculty senate leaders, legislators, teachers, principals, superintendents, students, alumni, parents, employers, and business and civic leaders.

These efforts helped to develop measures for the five goals included in *2020 Vision.* CPE has developed measures relating to students on such issues as access, enrollment, college readiness, retention, time to graduation, graduation rates, life-long learning, postcollege quality of life, postcollege career success, and postcollege civic and social roles. Other measures are institution-focused and include research dollar obtainment, space usage, employer satisfaction, position in rankings, and continuing education opportunities. An example of these measures on space utilization is the average weekly use of classroom and lab space and percentage occupancy per session.

While most of these measures have been fairly easy to develop, it is more difficult to measure the achievement of broader social goals. Furthermore, there has been disagreement within CPE about how to measure higher education quality. It is not easy to define the concept of quality in absolute terms, and CPE has not come to any agreement. Some elements of quality can be measured through the use of nationally normed tests. CPE is interested in using the concept of value-added, which considers the characteristics, skills, and values of students upon entry, not just absolute outcomes. CPE is also interested in "fitness for purpose," since there is not one single definition of quality that will work for all institutions. The search continues for measures both of quality and of the broader social goals contained in *2020 Vision*.

### *Evaluate Quality and Productivity Using Measures*

CPE measures the progress of the Kentucky higher-education system against national averages and similar information from other states. The council has a benchmark list of comparison institutions throughout the country for each university. Comparison with other states is the primary type of evaluation. Kentucky has expanded the list of states it compares its institutions to; the state wants to look beyond its traditional comparison states, such as Mississippi, Alabama, and Arkansas, to a group of states that includes North Carolina, Ohio, and Virginia. In addition, the evaluation also occurs through a self-comparison over time; Kentucky wants to see improvement on each measure over time.

# Appendix D: Balanced Scorecard

THE BALANCED SCORECARD IS A FRAMEWORK designed to help organizations translate their vision and mission statements into measurable performance goals and objectives while taking into account multiple perspectives, including customers, internal business processes, learning, and growth. Provider organizations use the balanced scorecard as an assessment tool primarily to identify goals and translate those goals into operational measures of performance. The balanced scorecard is associated primarily with Phase Two, Model Three.

Recognizing its value as a means to link short-term goals and objectives to long-term strategy, a wide range of organizations (including corporations, universities, nonprofit organizations, and government agencies) have adopted the balanced scorecard framework as a strategic management system. It is valued for its flexibility in implementation and reasonable requirement of time and resources and because it can be easily adapted to incorporate new initiatives in the organization.

The balanced scorecard is based on four main processes: translating the vision, communication and alignment, business planning, and feedback and learning. All four processes aim to create consistency and integration of priorities across the organization and to determine the right performance measurements. The translation of the vision is meant to create an understanding of the organization's vision through an "integrated set of objectives and measures that describe the long-term drivers of success" (Kaplan and Norton, 1996). The vision and strategy should then be communicated throughout the organization to ensure that departmental and individual employee goals and objectives are properly aligned with the long-term strategic vision. The business planning aspect links the budget to strategic planning and performance measurement, allowing decision makers to direct resources appropriately. Finally, the feedback and learning mechanism provides an opportunity for decision makers to review performance results and assess the validity of the organization's strategy and performance measures. The balanced scorecard places a heavy emphasis on continually updating strategy and measures to accurately reflect the changing operating environment.

Several government agencies, including the U.S. Customs Service, National Oceanic and Atmospheric Administration, Veterans Benefits Administration in the U.S. Department of Veterans Affairs, and the Department of Transportation, have recognized the benefits of the balanced scorecard framework in their efforts to comply with the Government Performance and Results Act (GPRA), which requires federal agencies to submit five-year strategic plans as well as annual performance plans with their budget requests to Congress. By helping agencies link their strategic planning with performance measurement objectives, the balanced scorecard organizes efforts across business lines so that processes and goals are aligned with the overall departmental strategy as required by GPRA.

The administrative offices of higher education institutions are also recognizing the value of the balanced scorecard, which serves the dual purpose of assessing for improvement and accountability. Offices in both the University of Southern California (USC) and the University of California at San Diego (UCSD) have incorporated the balanced scorecard as part of their larger efforts to improve the efficiency and effectiveness of their operations. Among other things, the balanced scorecard offers a way to streamline and prioritize activities as well as measure performance. Interestingly, the two schools are focusing on different aspects of their operations in their use of the scorecard; USC's Rossier School of Education is using the scorecard to measure academic quality, while UCSD's Business Affairs Office is focusing on measuring the productivity of its business operations.

# Phase One

The balanced scorecard is a technique used by providers for self-assessment. Phase One may be conducted by a provider, but not using this technique; thus, Phase One does not apply.

# Phase Two

The balanced scorecard is an example of an approach used in Model Three for provider-based self-assessment. The scorecard's emphasis on goal alignment, performance measurement, continuous improvement, and flexibility makes it an attractive option for self-assessment in organizations, particularly in contexts where involvement of multiple stakeholders is needed.

The balanced scorecard offers four perspectives from which to view the organization's effectiveness: financial, internal business, innovation and learning, and the customer. For each of these perspectives, the organization must first identify goals, then determine the measures and benchmarks that will capture the outcome of these goals.

### *Identify Goals for Education and Training*

For each of the four perspectives that orient the focus of the scorecard assessment, goals and corresponding measures must be determined. The scope and number of goals can change as the operating environment of the institution changes.

The Veterans Benefits Administration has used the scorecard to align its five diverse lines of business and found that three main factors were important in its successful implementation: consensus on the effort, a flexible structure, and effective communication.

The balanced scorecard allows the provider to include as many stakeholders as necessary in determining goals. For instance, the School of Education at USC developed its goals with a small committee consisting of two faculty administrators. The committee relied on the balanced scorecard as a way to focus on the department's goals for the next five years. Modifying the approach somewhat to fit the context of an academic institution, the committee developed an "academic scorecard" that includes no more than five goals for each scorecard perspective. Its goal selection process was based on current priorities of both the university and the department. The committee adopted many department-specific goals, mainly because in some instances university and department priorities did not match.

According to USC officials, the process of limiting the number of goals in each area imposed discipline on the committee and forced committee members to think about the organization's priorities. Not everything is equally important, and people have a tendency to associate importance with anything that is measured. Moreover, in a complex organization such as a university, different levels of bureaucracy often require different scorecards. For instance, campus security is an important goal for a university but not for a department. Some of the goals developed by the School of Education at USC are listed in Table D1.

**TABLE D1**
**USC School of Education Goals, by Perspective**

| Perspective | Goal |
| --- | --- |
| Academic management | Improve budget performance |
| | Improve school operations |
| | Improve management/leadership |
| Stakeholder | Quality of academic programs |
| | Student-centeredness |
| | Quality of faculty |
| | Value of money |
| | Alumni/employer satisfaction |
| Internal business | Improve faculty productivity |
| | Improve staff productivity |
| | Improve recruitment advisement |
| | Maintain responsibility to community |
| Innovation and learning | Improve quality of degree programs |
| | Increase student learning |
| | Improve quality of students |
| | Attract/keep talented faculty/staff |
| | Increase education innovation |
| | Faculty/staff development |

*Source:* O'Neil et al. (1999, p. 35).

### Develop Measures of Quality and Productivity

The balanced scorecard framework encourages institutions to identify a limited number of metrics that relate to the goals they have established. The Veterans Benefits Administration settled on speed, accuracy, cost, customer satisfaction, and employee development as the right performance measures for all the lines of business, although the measures are weighted differently for each area. The process of introducing the balanced scorecard and developing measures and performance goals was intended to be flexible and iterative, allowing "refinement in the measures and the organization to become familiar with the scorecard" (Williams and Wall, 1999, p. 1).

Selection of measures is not fixed, so different institutions can adopt different strategies. What affects selection are the requirements most important to the institution. In selecting measures, USC's School of Education has incorporated the use of benchmarks based on comparisons with other university graduate programs. It has also relied heavily on the *U.S. News & World Report* academic program rankings and set goals for improvement to match those institutions that are currently ranked in the top ten schools of education. USC's School of Education believes that the *U.S. News* rankings have a major influence on perception and "have become a de facto standard of excellence for prospective students and faculty" (O'Neil, Bensimon, Diamond, and Moore, 1999, p. 38). The measures have been based mainly on data already being collected regularly. Table D2 is an example of the goals, measures, and benchmarks for one of the perspectives included in the USC School of Education academic scorecard.

The UCSD Business Affairs Office has combined the balanced scorecard with the National Association of College and University Business Officers (NACUBO) benchmark program. NACUBO's benchmarking program was developed to "provide college and university administrators and managers with performance measurement information. . . . The program offers comparative operational performance data geared toward aiding administrators in sharing best practices and improving efficiency" (Shepko and Douglas, 1998). This component of UCSD's balanced scorecard enhances the usefulness of the balanced scorecard by informing the office not only about whether it is meeting its stated goals but also how it measures against comparable institutions.

## TABLE D2
## Stakeholder Perspective: How Do Stakeholders See Us? (USC)

| Goal | Measure | Benchmark |
|------|---------|-----------|
| Quality of academic programs | Ranking in *U.S. News and World Report* | Ascend to the top ten schools of education |
| | Teaching effectiveness | Equal average of top five of USC schools |
| Student-centeredness | Quality of student services is measured by student satisfaction with advisement, career development, job placement, course offerings, financial aid, etc. | |
| | School climate for special-population students, e.g., international, minority, and women | |
| Quality of faculty | Publications | Exceed average of publications per USC tenure-track faculty member |
| | Research funding | Equal average of top 11–20 in *U.S. News and World Report* |
| Value for money | Retention | Equal average of top five of USC graduate programs |
| | Reduced time to degree | Reduce time by 20 percent |
| | Return on student investment | Break even |
| Alumni satisfaction | To be developed | |
| Employer satisfaction | Quality of elementary and secondary school teachers | |

*Source:* O'Neil et al. (1999, p. 37).

The Business Affairs Office at UCSD implemented the scorecard in 1993 in response to fiscal problems and a changing business environment. As the office sought to introduce reengineered processes and operations in its lines of business, the balanced scorecard allowed it to focus efforts on where and when reengineering should be used. For each of the thirty core campus business functions, NACUBO benchmarks were selected to compare UCSD's performance in these areas with other research universities and participating University of California campuses (Relyea, 1998). Table D3 shows examples of business operations measured by the balanced scorecard and compared against benchmarks.

### Evaluate Quality and Productivity Using Measures

Evaluation relies on the comparison of performance with that of external peers (benchmarking). Indeed, the need to benchmark and the availability of such benchmarking information influences the choice of performance measures.

The process is continuous, with goals added or deleted as the operating environment changes. Once the scorecard has been completed, the organization must identify ways to implement it. At UCSD, results from the scorecard are the focus of an annual management retreat where leaders discuss the performance of the business functions against the benchmark institutions, "identified as either positive, neutral or negative. Negative performance gaps are addressed with an action plan" (Relyea, 1998). The business functions needing attention are then prioritized, an action plan is set, and goals are established for the following year. At USC, academic reviews are conducted every six years, and the scorecard framework for the USC School of Education currently is designed to fit this cycle. Scorecard information is mainly for internal use, but success stories are sometimes published for the benefit of others.

The scorecard can be successful if it attempts to desegregate the different aspects of an organization. In contrast, USC has not been able to undertake a systemwide effort to develop some of these indicators. Instead, the provost at USC is aggregating the lines of business by asking for "mindless" accountability through data inputs. Unfortunately, the university does not have a centralized office of research to move these efforts along.

## TABLE D3
## Examples of Business Operations Scorecard (UCSD)

| *Business Function* | *Measure* |
|---|---|
| *Internal Process Perspective: Are We Productive and Effective?* | |
| Administrative computing | Ratio of number of workstations to number of employees |
| | Ratio of technical employees in central organizations to number of technical employees |
| Benefits | Ratio of department cost to faculty staff head counter |
| | Ratio of faculty staff head counter to department FTE |
| Human resources | Ratio of HR cost to faculty staff head counter |
| | Ratio of faculty staff head counter to HR FTE |
| | Percentage of active career staff vested |
| | Percentage of career staff turnover |
| Housing | Ratio of number of bed spaces to department FTE |
| | Ratio of housing cost to bed space |
| Staff education and development | Ratio of course contract hours to staff FTE |
| | SE&D cost to staff FTE |
| *Innovation and Learning: How Do Our Employees Feel?* | |
| Administrative computing | Each business function rated on a 5-point scale on: |
| Admin. computing service | communication |
| Data center | compensation |
| | customer service |
| Benefits | decisionmaking |
| Human resources | diversity |
| Housing | leadership |
| Staff education and development | morale |
| | performance management |
| | teamwork |
| | training and development |
| | vision, values, mission |

*(Continued)*

## TABLE D3
## (*Continued*)

| Business Function | Measure |
|---|---|
| *Customer Perspective: How Do Our Customers See Us?* | |
| Administrative computing | 5-point satisfaction scale; surveyed academic and administrative staff separately |
| Benefits | 5-point satisfaction scale; surveyed academic and administrative staff separately |
| Human resources | None |
| Housing | 5-point student satisfaction scores |
| Staff education and development | 5-point satisfaction scale; surveyed academic and administrative staff separately |
| *Financial Perspective: How Do We Look to Resource Providers?* | |
| Administrative computing | None |
| Benefits | None |
| Human resources | None |
| Housing | Profitability and efficiency ratios |
| Staff education and development | None |

*Note:* See www.vcba.ucsd.edu/performance/.

The whole point of the balanced scorecard is for managers to select high-level indicators that can help them monitor progress toward key goals. Thus, the results of the balanced scorecard should be linked to the general management of the organization. Implications can be broad or narrow, depending on how comprehensive the framework is.

# Appendix E: Certifiers of Student Competencies

CERTIFIERS OF STUDENT competencies are intermediaries in the education and professional development process, even if they happen to provide education as well. Their purpose is to certify that students have achieved a clearly defined level of knowledge, skill, ability, expertise, or aptitude. The focus of assessment is on the learner rather than the provider.

In competency-based education and training, where the certifier also provides education, assessment (including the design of assessment instruments) is often integrated into the education and training activities. Curriculum development is closely linked to and even driven by the definition of competencies and the operationalization of those competencies in the assessment instruments.

In recent years, there has been increased attention focused on the concept of student competencies by government, business leaders, and educators as an innovative approach to education and training, as well as assessment. Competency-based assessment focuses on individual student outcomes and operationalizes the specified competencies and helps determine where instruction is needed (Pottinger and Goldsmith, 1979). This allows educators to organize courses and instruction around the gap between what students already know and what they should know to demonstrate a level of proficiency in a particular area.

Competency-based education benefits students because it gives them recognition of past achievements, portability of course credits, and a system for lifelong learning (Paulson and Ewell, 1999). Institutions value competency-based education and training because they encourage stakeholders to closely examine what is important for students to know and instructors to teach as well as target scarce resources where they will be most effective (Mager, 1997).

## Phase One

When the certification of student competencies is conducted by a system-level intermediary, there is substantial overlap between Phase One assessment and the process of identifying goals in Phase Two. However, if the certification of student competencies is conducted by a provider serving many customers, then Phase One will normally be conducted by the customer or stakeholder (if at all), while Phase Two is conducted by the provider. Because the latter example is more common in the education and professional development arena, we discuss the approaches used to define goals in terms of Phase Two assessment here. Many of the techniques described here could also be used in Phase One by a system-level certifier interested in a Model Four approach.

## Phase Two

Competency-based education and professional development provides examples of Model Four assessment approach.

### *Identify Goals for Education and Training*
The competencies identified as critical to a customer or other stakeholder embody the goals of education and professional development.

There are different ideas about how to define competencies. The most common method is to identify tasks and a definition of their successful accomplishment that define competency in a certain domain. Critics argue that this oversimplifies performance in the real world by ignoring the relationship between tasks and other factors that influence performance. Another approach to competency definition looks only at general characteristics needed for effective job performance—for example, critical thinking skills or communication skills. This method of competency definition ignores the need for different skills in different domains and that

> *individuals demonstrate little capacity to transfer expertise from one area to another . . . and [this] provides limited help for those involved in the practical work of designing education and training programs for specific professions (Gonczi, 1994, p. 29).*

A more integrated approach combines defined tasks and cross-cutting skills to define the knowledge, skills, and abilities needed to perform effectively in particular domain areas. In this approach, "competence is conceived of as complex structuring of attributes needed for intelligent performance in specific situations" (ibid.).

The steps involved in defining competencies are a "reverse engineering" process where jobs are broken down, organized into domains, and an assessment system developed around them. Most approaches begin with a job analysis and the decomposition of roles by defining what an individual should be able to do under particular circumstances. These performance descriptions should be developed by all the stakeholders who have an interest in the degree or certification being awarded. Performance descriptions should be specific to the institution and degree and specified as valid for a determined time period (Paulson and Ewell, 1999).

The next step involves "chunking" or grouping the competencies into domains and subdomains, rather than just producing a laundry list of tasks that individuals should be able to perform. This step allows flexibility in awarding degrees and credentials because students can focus on subareas and earn lower-level certifications without having to complete an entire sequence of courses that may not be useful to them. This allows institutions to serve the wide-ranging needs of a diverse student body.

The federal government has recognized the benefits of conducting job analysis to identify the necessary competencies for certain jobs. The Department of Labor Secretary's Commission on Achieving Necessary Skills (SCANS) initiative was undertaken with the intent of linking competencies and skills needed by the business community and government to what is taught in schools.

SCANS aims to "define the skills needed for employment, propose acceptable levels of proficiency, suggest effective ways to assess proficiency and develop a dissemination strategy" (U.S. Department of Labor, 1991, p. xv). The SCANS team had meetings and discussions with business and government leaders, created six special panels, and commissioned researchers to conduct interviews throughout the business sector. The competencies and foundation skills that they identified are based on an analysis of 15 jobs,

> *through detailed, in-depth interviews, lasting up to four hours each, with job holders or their supervisors. The interviews explored the general job description, confirmed ratings of the importance of skills, and inquired about "critical incidents" and illustrative tasks and tools used on the job (U.S. Department of Labor, 1991, D-1).*

While SCANS acknowledges that technical expertise varies between industries, it posits that the basic competencies or "workplace know-how" is the same for all types of jobs. SCANS identified five major categories of skills that are needed in all industries: resources, interpersonal, information, systems, and technology. In addition, according to SCANS, students need a three-part foundation consisting of basic skills, thinking skills, and personal qualities.

Private industry has also acknowledged the benefits of identifying competencies. American College Testing (ACT) has developed a program called Work Keys, which is a system employers use in hiring to determine how candidates match job requirements and where they need training.

Using SkillPro (ACT proprietary software), an analyst develops a list of tasks most relevant to the job under review using company information, job descriptions, and the Dictionary of Occupational Titles. It is then revised and amended by experienced employees who decide which tasks are most critical to the job. This is followed by an assessment of which Work Keys skills are relevant and at what level they are needed for the job. The desired skill level is determined "on both importance (significance of task to overall job performance) and relative time spent (compared to other tasks)" (ACT, 1997). ACT also conducts assessments of current skill levels in up to eight critical areas: reading for information, applied mathematics, applied technology, teamwork, listening, locating information, observation, and writing. In addition, Work Keys includes an instructional support component to help educators assist students/learners improve their workplace skills. ACT also developed a series of guides called *Targets for Instruction* that give

> *detailed descriptions of particular skill areas and of characteristics that distinguish each skill level. The targets are designed as spring-boards for building curricula and training materials tailored to the specific needs of the client (ACT, 1997, p. 8).*

Work Keys is used in a wide variety of industries including technology, manufacturing, service, and retail. ACT has profiled over 5,000 jobs in both white- and blue-collar occupations (ACT, 1997).

### Develop Measures of Quality and Productivity

Competency-based education uses student tests as a measure of performance. These tests may be traditional standardized, paper-and-pencil or computer-based tests (such as state licensing examinations or tests sponsored by ACT) or tests that require a learner to demonstrate a skill in a practical setting.

The organization of competencies into domains and subdomains also aids in the process of developing measures by distinguishing between job-specific competencies and more generic skills. The skills can be categorized separately, allowing assessments to be customized for a wide range of degree and certification types using the cross-cutting skill assessments to augment the profession-specific measurement tools (Paulson and Ewell, 1999).

### Evaluate Quality and Productivity Using Measures

As described previously, the development of measures and evaluation of performance follows directly from the process of identifying goals (i.e., identifying competencies). The defined competencies reflect the desired endpoint—what is required of students to know or do. Performance measures are designed to reflect how much they know or how much they can do. Normally, performance is compared to some objective standard or desired end state that is specified in the process of identifying the goals of education and professional development.

The competency-based evaluation method is appealing because it " . . . enables us to come closer than we have in the past to assessing what we want to assess—the capacity of the professional to integrate knowledge, values, attitudes and skills in the world of practice" (Gonczi, 1994, p. 28).

It requires an integrated approach because knowledge, skills, and attitudes are closely connected in their influence on job performance. Such evaluations not only "directly test performance but also suggest how individual knowledge and skill elements should be combined" (Paulson and Ewell, 1999, p. 10). To the extent that competency-based assessment is a tool for measuring the need for instruction, it is also a tool for determining when education or training is not necessary. A variety of methods should be employed in competency-based assessment and efforts made to evaluate performance directly in real-world situations when feasible (Gonczi, 1994). It is, however, time consuming and expensive to go through this process, and to update the competencies and the assessment mechanisms. In addition, many observers are skeptical that a competency-based education approach will be embraced by the academic community (Carnevale, 2000).

**Example: The Western Governors University.** The Western Governors University (WGU), established in 1997, has been a leader in higher education's competency-based approach to education. The university was created to address several challenges, including

> a wide geographic dispersion of students; non-traditional students, such as adults employed full time, seeking part-time enrollment; scarcity of workers in certain highly trained occupations; rising student costs of attaining higher education; existing and potential duplication of effort among states in developing courses and programs; failure of existing higher educational institutions to recognize and acknowledge skills and abilities which students already possess; and inadequate information to students about educational opportunities and choices (Testa, 1999, p. 3).

WGU differs from traditional institutions of higher education in that the degree and certificate programs[17] are defined by a set of competencies that students must demonstrate rather than a set of courses they must take. Thus, WGU's primary effort is directed toward defining an appropriate set of competencies, developing valid and reliable methods for measuring those competencies, and helping students identify learning opportunities that can help them acquire competencies they are lacking. The attainment of a degree or certificate is not based on credit hours but the successful completion of a set of competency tests. In fact, students may earn a degree or certification without taking courses if they can demonstrate competency in a domain area (ibid.).

WGU faculty plays a key role in the design and development of programs and tests designed to assess performance. Actual courses are delivered by distance learning providers, which are approved by WGU for providing education that fosters the development of specific competencies. Programs are developed through analysis, research, competency and assessment development, content identification, implementation, and a review and evaluation process. The research and analysis portion of program development ensures that there is a demand in the proposed subject area, both by students and the job market, and information is collected on content, providers, and assessment.

The competencies are developed by special program councils composed of experts in the field. The council members come together to identify the required "knowledge, skills and abilities" (KSAs) that students would be required to demonstrate within a discrete area of competence" (ibid., p. 5). These KSAs are organized into domains and more-detailed subdomains of competencies required for a degree or certificate. In developing competency statements, council members consider the target audience, including their educational and skill level; characteristics of the students enrolled in the program (adult, full- or part-time); the types of jobs that the degree or certification may lead to; and finally, the types of skills and abilities that should be demonstrated by successful graduates.

The WGU appoints an assessment council for "overall oversight for the development, approval and delivery of WGU assessments" (ibid., p. 8). The assessment council works with the program council to ensure that assessments are appropriate for the competencies being measured.

# Appendix F: On-line Sources

| | |
|---|---|
| Accreditation Board of Engineering and Technology | www.abet.org |
| Accreditation Council on Continuing Medical Education | www.accme.org |
| Accreditation Council for Graduate Medical Education | www.acgme.org |
| American Bar Association | www.abanet.org |
| American College Testing | www.act.org/workkeys/index.html |
| American Dental Association | www.ada.org |
| American Medical Accreditation Program | www.ama-assn.org/med-sci/amapsite/index.htm |
| American Medical Association | www.ama-assn.org |
| American Psychological Association | www.apa.org |
| American Society for Training and Development | www.astd.org |
| Annual Data Profile for Public Community and Technical Colleges of Texas | www.thecb.state.tx.us/ctc/perfdata/default.htm |
| Association of Universities in the Netherlands | www.vsnu.nl |
| Berkeley Extension | www.unex.berkeley.edu |
| City University of New York–Queens College | www.qc.edu |

| | |
|---|---|
| College Profiles for Public Community and Technical Colleges of Texas | www.thecb.state.tx.us/reports/pdf/ 0444.pdf |
| Department of Agriculture | www.usda.gov |
| Department of Education | www.ed.gov |
| Department of Transportation | www.dot.gov |
| The European Commission on Education, Training, and Youth | europa.eu.int/comm/dgs/ education_culture/index_en.htm |
| Forest Service | www.fs.fed.us |
| H-530.947 AMA Structure, Governance, and Operations | www.ama-assn.org |
| Harvard Extension | extension.dce.harvard.edu |
| Health and Human Services | www.hhs.gov |
| Institutional Effectiveness Measures and Standards: On-Site Review for Texas Community and Technical Colleges | www.thecb.state.tx.us/ctc/ie/ default.htm |
| Liaison Committee on Medical Education | www.lcme.org |
| Michigan State University | www.msue.msu.edu |
| National Association of College and University Business Officers | www.nacubo.org |
| New England Association of Schools and Colleges, Inc., Standards for Accreditation | www.neasc.org/cihe/stancihe.htm |
| North Central Association of Colleges and Schools Commission on Institutions of Higher Education | www.ncacihe.org/mission/index.html |
| Praxiom Research Group Limited | www.connect.ab.ca/~praxiom/ intro.htm |
| The Quality Assurance Agency for Higher Education | www.qaa.ac.uk |

| | |
|---|---|
| Social Security Administration | www.ssa.gov |
| South Carolina Commission for Higher Education | www.che400.state.sc.us |
| Stanford Extension | continuingstudies.stanford.edu |
| Tennessee Board of Regents | www.tbr.state.tn.us |
| Texas Higher Education Institutional Effectiveness | www.thecb.state.tx.us/ctc/ie |
| UCLA Extension | www.unex.ucla.edu |
| United States House of Representatives Majority Leader | freedom.house.gov |
| United States Postal Service | www.usps.gov |
| University of Massachusetts at Amherst | www.umass.edu |
| University of Phoenix | www.phoenix.edu |
| University of Texas at Austin | www.utexas.edu/cee |
| Western Governors University | www.wgu.edu |

# Notes

[1]The discussion of the role of intermediaries is based on theoretical work on the role of intermediaries as well as real-world examples of intermediaries that fill an unmet need in a system. The theoretical literature focuses on information asymmetry between providers and customers and discusses scenarios under which intermediary organizations might emerge, conditions under which intermediaries can provide useful information, and the roles they play in providing useful information to consumers or ensuring minimum standards of quality in the marketplace. See Biglaiser and Friedman, 1994; Biglaiser, 1993; Lizzeri, 1999; Leland, 1979; and Avery, Resnick, and Zeckhauser, 1999, for more details. Examples of other roles for intermediaries emerge from various references, including Meister, 1998; McGuinness, 1997; Stevens and Hamlett, 1983; Master Plan Survey Team, 1960; U.S. Department of Transportation, 1997a, 1997b.

[2]In 1947, the International Organization for Standardization (ISO) developed common international product standards to enhance international commerce. Forty years later, the ISO created a management strategy referred to as *ISO 9000,* as well as ISO 9001, 9002, 9003, and 9004. ISO 9000 and 9004 are guidelines (ISO 9000 is generally used to guide an organization in the choice of standards it should use, whereas ISO 9004 provides information about implementing and using the guidelines), while ISO 9001, 9002, and 9003 are three separate contractual standards used to certify an organization as ISO compliant (Mendel, 2000). Together, these guidelines and standards are designed to ensure that an organization is implementing and adhering to standardized quality production.

[3]Many systems do not view this type of misalignment as a problem. For example, some companies might support training and education that benefits the employees as individuals (e.g., enrichment courses), even if it does not relate to their jobs. Similarly, state institutions of higher education often offer courses or sponsor research that is not of direct interest to the state.

[4]Every military and civilian job in the Air Force is associated with a functional Air Force Specialty Code (AFSC), which is in turn part of a career field. Each career field has a high-level manager—a person who is in charge of the enlisted, officer, and civilian workforce in that functional area. Among other things, that individual is responsible for the training and education of individuals in that career field. The career field manager is in the Pentagon (functional headquarters) or in a specific command (when the specialty is confined to one major command).

[5]Models One, Two, and Three reflect traditional approaches to educational assessment that focus on the provider and implicitly assume that if the institution is good, students who pass through the institution have learned what they needed to learn. Indeed, many provider-based assessments consider evidence of student performance, improvement, or achievement (e.g., pass rates on licensure exams) as a measure of an institution's success or failure. In that respect, information on student performance can be an element of all four assessment models. What makes Model Four different from the others is that the assessment essentially ignores the provider. In fact, an individual need not attend a course to achieve certification. Instead, he or she may learn skills or concepts on the job, through a CD-ROM, or be self-taught. What further complicates the distinction between Model Four and provider-based assessment is the fact that many professional societies require that individuals both graduate from an institution that is accredited by the society and pass a licensing examination to be certified as a professional in that field. In other words, these professional societies require that both the individual competencies be assessed through Model Four and that the providers be assessed, normally through a Model Two–style assessment process.

[6]There are six accreditation regions in the United States: Middle States, New England, North Central, Northwest, Southern, and Western. Generally, each region has a regional accreditation commission, but two of the regions (Western and New England) have two separate organizations: one in charge of accreditation for two-year colleges and one for four-year colleges.

[7]Resource dependence theory (Pfeffer and Salancik, 1978; Greening and Gray, 1994; Heimovics, Herman, and Jurkiewicz Coughlin, 1993) also specifies that an organization will be less likely to resist external pressures when it is dependent on the sources of those pressures. An example of this theory is found in higher education state boards. Some of these boards control funding for new programs; therefore, institutions are likely to comply with a board's vision, values, and mandates when creating new programs to secure funding.

[8]One might ask whether an ideal authority relationship exists for promoting assessment. Unfortunately, the definition of a good assessment system depends on the objectives to be achieved by the assessment system. There are many different stakeholders in any education system, and different stakeholders often have different goals and objectives. For example, a system in which the state higher education board has a high level of authority over the institutions of higher education in the state might be viewed as highly effective from the

point of view of the governor, state legislators, and taxpayers. But the institutions, faculty, and students might view such a system as detrimental to the quality of higher education.

[9]The assessment literature formerly emphasized a distinction between outputs and outcomes. Outputs reflect what is produced by the education activity, whereas outcomes reflect the overall impact of the education and professional development and relate more closely to the goals of education and professional development. Outputs are normally stated in terms of numbers: the number of students served, the number of graduates, and so on. Outcomes are much more general and can include the impact of the learning experience on the learner's job performance or lifetime income. The literature now tends to refer to both outputs and outcomes as outcomes, because both are closely related to goals and can be understood as outcomes of the educational process. We have adopted that convention in the text of this report.

[10]Serban (1998b) reports that most states use a combination of comparisons with historical, peer, and preset data.

[11]We conducted a thorough search of online bibliographic reference materials related to corporate universities, professional education and training, and related evaluation practices. Relevant sources were retrieved from the Management Contents, ABI/Inform, PsycInfo, ERIC, and Business Periodicals Index databases. In our review, we gave highest priority to academic and professional society publications because of their attention to study methods and generalizability of results.

In addition, members of the project team attended the Corporate Universities 2000: Benchmarks for the New Millennium conference organized by Corporate University Xchange, Inc., in April 2000, where a range of corporate learning organizations presented their learning and development activities.

[12]These findings from our site visits and literature review parallel those reported in an earlier Annual Review of Psychology article by Tannenbaum and Yukl (1992).

[13]This appendix is based primarily on a conversation with and briefing given by Learning and Performance Center Vice President Bill Harrod.

[14]*Lucent Magazine*, March/April 2000, pp. 14–17.

[15]See Education Commission of the States (1997) or Appendix C for a complete description of the distinction between coordinating and governing boards.

[16]Each university and community or technical college in the state has its own governing board.

[17]WGU is currently a candidate for accreditation. Current degree programs offered include a general AA, an AAS in electronics manufacturing engineering, an AAS in information technology, and an MA in learning and technology. WGU is building a bachelor's degree in business.

# References

Adelman, C. (2000). A parallel universe. *Change, 32*(3), 20–30.

Albright, B. N. (1995). The accountability litmus test: Long-term performance improvement with contained costs. In G. H. Gaither (Ed.), *Assessing performance in an age of accountability: Case studies* (pp. 65–76). New Directions for Higher Education, no. 91. San Francisco: Jossey-Bass.

Alstete, J. W. (1995). *Benchmarking in higher education: Adapting best practices to improve quality.* ASHE-ERIC Higher Education Report (vol. 24, no. 5). Washington, DC: Graduate School of Education and Human Development, The George Washington University.

American College Testing. (1997). *Work keys: Targets for instruction.* Iowa City: American College Testing.

American Productivity and Quality Center, Institute for Education Best Practices. (1987). *Measuring institutional performance outcomes.* Final report. Houston: American Productivity and Quality Center.

American Psychological Association. (1985). *Standards for educational and psychological testing.* Washington, DC: American Psychological Association.

American Society for Quality Control Standards Committee. (1996). *Quality assurance standards: Guidelines for the application of ANSI/ISO/ASQC Q9001 or Z9002 to education and training institutions.* Milwaukee: American Society for Quality Control.

Aper, J. P., Cuver, S. M., and Hinkle, D. E. (1990). Coming to terms with the accountability versus improvement debate in assessment. *Higher Education, 20,* 471–483.

Aper, J. P., and Hinkle, D. E. (1991). State policies for assessing student outcomes: A case study with implications for state and institutional authorities. *Journal of Higher Education, 62,* 539–555.

Association of American Colleges, Project on Redefining the Meaning and Purpose of Baccalaureate Degrees. (1985). *Integrity in the college curriculum: A report to the academic community.* Washington, DC: Association of American Colleges.

Avery, C., Resnick, P., and Zeckhauser, R. (1999). The market for evaluations. *American Economic Review, 89,* 564–584.

Babbie, E. (1992). *The practice of social research*. Belmont, CA: Wadsworth Publishing Company.

Banta, T. W. (1988). Assessment as an instrument of state funding policy. In T. W. Banta (Ed.), *Implementing outcomes assessment: Promise and perils* (pp. 81–94). New Directions for Institutional Research, no. 59. San Francisco: Jossey-Bass.

Banta, T. W., and Borden, V.M.H. (1994). Performance indicators for accountability and improvement. In V.M.H. Borden and T. W. Banta (Eds.), *Using performance indicators to guide strategic decision making* (pp. 95–106). New Directions for Institutional Research, no. 82. San Francisco: Jossey-Bass.

Bassi, L. J. (2000, May). *Measuring ROI: The business of learning*. Proceedings from the Post-Conference Workshop of Corporate Universities 2000: Benchmarks for a New Millennium, Las Vegas, NV.

Bassi, L. J., and Van Buren, M. (1999). Sharpening the leading edge. *Training and Development, 53*(1), 23–28.

Benjamin, R., and others. (2000). *Achieving the Texas higher education vision*. Santa Monica, CA: RAND.

Bennett, W. J. (1984). *To reclaim a legacy: A report on the humanities in higher education*. Washington, DC: National Endowment for the Humanities.

Biglaiser, G. (1993). Middlemen as experts. *RAND Journal of Economics, 24,* 212–223.

Biglaiser, G., and Friedman, J. (1994). Middlemen as guarantors of quality. *International Journal of Industrial Organization, 12,* 509–531.

Borden, V.M.H., and Bottrill, K. V. (1994). Performance indicators: History, definitions, and methods. In V.M.H. Borden and T. W. Banta (Eds.), *Using performance indicators to guide strategic decision making* (pp. 5–21). New Directions for Institutional Research, no. 82. San Francisco: Jossey-Bass.

Boyer, C., Ewell, P., Finney, J., and Mingle, J. (1987). Assessment and outcomes measurement: A view from the states. *AAHE Bulletin, 39*(7), 8–12.

California State Department of Education, Master Plan Survey Team. (1960). *A master plan for higher education in California, 1960–1975*. Sacramento: California State Department of Education.

Cambridge, B., and others. (Eds.). (2001). Electronic portfolios: Emerging practices in student, faculty, and institutional learning. Washington, DC: American Association for Higher Education.

Campbell, D. T., and Fiske, D. W. (1959). Convergent and discriminant validation by the multitrait-multimethod matrix. *Psychological Bulletin, 15,* 546–553.

Campbell, D. T., and Stanley, J. C. (1966). *Experimental and quasi-experimental designs for research*. Chicago: Rand McNally.

Carnevale, D. (2000, May 19). Two models for collaboration in distance learning. *Chronicle of Higher Education*. (www.chronicle.com)

Cavalluzzo, L. C., and Cymrot, D. J. (1998). *A bottom-up assessment of Navy flagship schools (CRM 97–24)*. Alexandria, VA: Center for Naval Analyses.

Chickering, A., and Gamson, Z. (Eds.). (1991). *Applying the seven principles for good practice in undergraduate education*. San Francisco: Jossey-Bass.

Cole, H. P., and others. (1984). *Measuring learning in continuing education for engineers and scientists.* Phoenix, AZ: Oryx Press.

Cole, J.J.K., Nettles, M. T., and Sharp, S. (1997). Assessment of teaching and learning for improvement and accountability: State governing, coordinating board and regional accreditation association policies and practices. Ann Arbor: National Center for Postsecondary Improvement, University of Michigan.

Cook, T. D., and Campbell, D. T. (1979). Quasi-experimentation: Design and analysis issues for field settings. Chicago: Rand McNally.

Council for Higher Education Accreditation. (2000, January 24–26). *2000 Annual Conference: Quality assurance—Distance learning and international perspectives and needs,* Washington, DC.

Cronbach, L. J. (1971). Test validation. In R. L. Thorndike (Ed.), *Educational measurement* (2nd ed., pp. 443–507). Washington, DC: American Council on Education.

Cronbach, L. J., and Gleser, G. C. (1965). *Psychological tests and personnel decisions* (2nd ed.). Urbana: University of Illinois Press.

Dickinson, T. L., and Hedge, J. W. (1989). *WCRK performance ratings: Measurement test bed for validity and accuracy research.* Interim Technical Paper for Period June 1985–September 1987. AFHRL–TP–88–36. San Antonio, TX: Training Systems Division, Brooks Air Force Base.

Dill, D. (2000a). Designing academic audits: Lessons learned in Europe and Asia. *Quality in Higher Education, 6*(3), 187–207.

Dill, D. (2000b). www.unc.edu/courses/acaudit/whatisacademicaudit.html.

Easton, D. (1965). *A Framework for Political Analysis.* Englewood Cliffs, NJ: Prentice Hall.

Education Commission of the States. (1997). *1997 state postsecondary education structures sourcebook: State coordinating and governing boards.* Denver: Education Commission of the States.

El-Khawas, E. (1995). *Campus trends 1995.* Higher Education Panel Report No. 85. Washington, DC: American Council on Education.

Epstein, P. (1992). Measuring the performance of public services. In M. Holzer (Ed.), *Public productivity handbook.* New York: Marcel Dekker.

Ewell, P. T. (1987a). *Assessment, accountability, and improvement: Managing the contradiction.* Boulder, CO: National Center for Higher Education Management Systems.

Ewell, P. T. (1987b). Assessment: Where are we? The implications of new state mandates. *Change, 19*(1), 23–28.

Ewell, P. T. (1990). *State policy on assessment: The linkage to learning.* Denver: Education Commission of the States.

Ewell, P. T. (1991). Assessment and public accountability: Back to the future. *Change, 23*(6), 12–17.

Ewell, P. T. (1993). The role of states and accreditors in shaping assessment practice. In T. W. Banta (Ed.), *Making a difference: Outcomes of a decade of assessment in higher education* (pp. 339–356). San Francisco: Jossey-Bass.

Ewell, P. T. (1999a). Assessment of higher education and quality: Promise and politics. In S. J. Messick (Ed.), *Assessment in higher education: Issues of access, quality, student development, and public policy.* Mahwah, NJ: Erlbaum.

Ewell, P. T. (1999b). *A delicate balance: The role of evaluation in management.* Boulder, CO: National Center for Higher Education Management Systems.

Ewell, P. T., and Wellman, J. (1997). *Refashioning accountability: Toward a "coordinated" system of quality assurance for higher education.* Policy Papers on Higher Education. Denver: Education Commission of the States. (ED 410 812)

Gardiner, L. F. (1994). *Redesigning higher education: Producing dramatic gains in student learning.* ASHE-ERIC Higher Education Report (vol. 23, no. 7). Washington, DC: Graduate School of Education and Human Development, The George Washington University.

Gilmore, J. L., and To, D. (1992). Evaluating academic productivity and quality. In C. S. Hollins (Ed.), *Containing costs and improving productivity in higher education.* San Francisco: Jossey-Bass.

Gonczi, A. (1994). Competency-based assessment in the professions in Australia. *Assessment in Education, 1*(1), 27–44.

Gray, G.R.H., McKenzie, E., Miller, M., and Shasky, C. (1997). Training practices in state government agencies. *Public Personnel Management, 26*(2), 187–202.

Greening, D. W., and Gray, B. (1994). Testing a model of organizational response to social and political issues. *Academy of Management Journal,* 467–498.

Hebel, S. (1999, May 28). Government and politics: Virginia board wants to link state aid for colleges to their performance in key areas. *Chronicle of Higher Education.* (www.chronicle.com)

Heimovics, R. D., Herman, R. D., and Jurkiewicz Coughlin, C. L. (1993). Executive leadership and resource dependence in nonprofit organizations: A frame analysis. *Public Administration Review, 53,* 419–427.

Holton, E.F.I. (1996). New employee development: A review and reconceptualization. *Human Resource Development Quarterly, 7*(3), 233–252.

Houston, G.R.J. (1992). Achieving productivity gains in financial management. In R. E. Anderson and J. W. Meyerson (Eds.), *Productivity and higher education: Improving the effectiveness of faculty, facilities, and financial resources* (pp. 85–93). Princeton, NJ: Peterson's Guides.

Hutchins, G. (1993). *ISO 9000: A comprehensive guide to registration, audit guidelines, and successful certification.* Bases Junction, VT: Oliver Wright.

Izadi, M., Ali, K. E., and Stadt, R. W. (1996). Quality in higher education: Lessons learned from the Baldrige Award, Deming Prize, and ISO 9000 registration. *Journal of Industrial Teacher Education, 33*(2), 60–76.

Jacobi, M., Astin, A., and Ayala, F. (1987). *College student outcomes assessment: A talent development perspective.* ASHE-ERIC Higher Education Report, no. 7. Washington, DC: Association for the Study of Higher Education.

Joint Staff for the Committee. (1957). *A study of the need for additional centers of public higher education in California.* Sacramento: California State Department of Education.

Kaplan, R. S., and Norton, D. (1996). Using the balanced scorecard as a strategic management system. *Harvard Business Review, 74*(1), 75–85.

Kirkpatrick, D. L. (1998). *Evaluating training programs: The four levels.* San Francisco: Berrett-Koehler.

Leland, H. (1979). Quacks, lemons, and licensing: A theory of minimum quality standards. *Journal of Political Economy, 87,* 1328–1346.

Lenth, C. S. (1996). What political leaders expect from postsecondary assessment. In National Center for Higher Education Management Systems, *The national assessment of college student learning: An inventory of state-level assessment activities* (pp. 157–164). Boulder, CO: National Center for Higher Education Management Systems.

Levy, D., and others. (2001). Strategic and performance planning for the office of the chancellor for education and professional development. Santa Monica, CA: RAND.

Light, R. J., Singer, J. D., and Willett, J. B. (1990). *By design: Planning research on higher education.* Cambridge, MA: Harvard University Press.

Lively, K. (1999, February 26). Money and management: U. of Florida's "bank" rewards colleges that meet key goals. *Chronicle of Higher Education.* (www.chronicle.com)

Lizzeri, A. (1999). Information revelation and certification intermediaries. *RAND Journal of Economics, 30,* 214–231.

Mager, R. F. (1997). *Preparing instructional objectives.* Atlanta: Center for Effective Performance.

Mann, R. B. (1996–97). Seven questions to ask before investing in a training program. *Small Business Forum, 14*(3), 50–60.

Massy, W. F. (1994). Measuring performance: How colleges and universities can set meaningful goals and be accountable. In J. W. Meyerson and W. F. Massy (Eds.), *Measuring institutional performance in higher education* (pp. 29–54). Princeton, NJ: Peterson's Guides.

Massy, W. F., and French, N. (1997, May). *Teaching and learning quality process review: A review of the Hong Kong program.* Paper presented at the International Network for Quality Assurance Agencies in Higher Education.

Massy, W. F., and French, N. (1999, May). *Teaching and learning quality process review: What has the programme achieved in Hong Kong?* Paper presented at the International Network for Quality Assurance Agencies in Higher Education.

McGuinness, A. C., Jr. (1997). *The functions and evaluations of state coordination and governance in postsecondary education.* Denver: National Center for Postsecondary Management Systems.

Meister, J. C. (1998). *Corporate universities: Lessons in building a world class work force.* New York: McGraw-Hill.

Mendel, P. (2000). Global models of organization: International management standards, reforms, and movements. Unpublished dissertation proposal, Stanford University.

Messick, S. (1975). The standard problem: Meaning and values in measurement and evaluation. *American Psychologist, 30,* 955–966.

Messick, S. (1989). Validity. In R. L. Linn (Ed.), *Educational measurement* (3rd ed.). New York: Macmillan.

Messick, S. (1996). Validity of performance assessments. In G. Phillips (Ed.), *Technical issues in large-scale performance assessment* (pp. 1–18). NCES-802. Washington, DC: U.S. Department of Education, Office of Educational Research and Improvement.

National Center for Higher Education Management Systems. (1996). *The national assessment of college student learning: An inventory of state-level assessment activities.* Boulder, CO: National Center for Higher Education Management Systems.

National Institute of Education. (1984). *Involvement in learning: Realizing the potential of American higher education.* Washington, DC: National Institute of Education.

National Institute for Standards and Technology, Baldrige National Quality Program. (1995). *Malcolm Baldrige National Quality Award: 1995 criteria.* Gaithersburg, MD: National Institute for Standards and Technology.

National Institute for Standards and Technology, Baldrige National Quality Program. (1999). *Education criteria for performance excellence.* Gaithersburg, MD: National Institute for Standards and Technology. (www.quality.nist.gov)

Nunnally, J. C. (1970). *Introduction to psychological measurement.* New York: McGraw-Hill.

Office of Management and Budget. (1998). *Preparation and submission of strategic plans and annual performance plans.* Circular A-11, Part 2. Washington DC: Office of Management and Budget.

Oliver, C. (1991). Strategic responses to institutional processes. *Academy of Management Review, 16,* 145–179.

O'Neil, H., Bensimon, E., Diamond, M., and Moore, M. (1999, November/December). Designing and implementing an academic scorecard. *Change,* 34–40.

Ory, J. C. (1991). Suggestions for deciding between commercially available and locally developed assessment instruments. *North Central Association Quarterly, 66*(2), 451–457.

Palomba, C. A., and Banta, T. W. (1999). *Assessment essentials: Planning, implementing, and improving assessment in higher education.* San Francisco: Jossey-Bass.

Paulson, K., and Ewell, P. (1999). *21st century skills for community college education: The critical role of competencies.* Boulder, CO: National Center for Higher Education Management Systems.

Pfeffer, J., and Salancik, G. (1978). *The external control of organizations: A resource dependence perspective.* New York: Harper & Row.

Phillips, J. J. (1997). A rational approach to evaluating training programs . . . including calculating ROI. *Journal of Lending and Credit Risk Management, 79*(11), 43–50.

Pottinger, P. S., and Goldsmith, J. (Eds.). (1979). *Defining and measuring competence.* San Francisco: Jossey-Bass.

Reisberg, L. (2000, August 28). Assailed substance of *U.S. News* college rankings. *Chronicle of Higher Education.* (www.chronicle.com)

Relyea, S. W. (1998). From gutter balls to strikes. *NACUBO Business Officer.* Washington, DC: National Association of College and University Business Officers. (www.nacubo.org/website/members/bomag/9806/scorecard.html)

Richardson, R. (1994). Illinois. In S. Ruppert (Ed.), *Charting higher education accountability: A sourcebook on state-level performance indicators.* Denver: Education Commission of the States.

Richardson, R., Bracco, K., Callan, P., and Finney, J. (1999). *Designing State Higher Education Systems for a New Century.* Phoenix, AZ: The Oryx Press.

Ruppert, S. S. (1995). Roots and realities of state-level performance indicator systems. In G. H. Gaither (Ed.), *Assessing performance in an age of accountability: Case studies* (pp. 11–23). New Directions for Higher Education, no. 91. San Francisco: Jossey-Bass.

Schapiro, M. O. (1993). The concept of productivity as applied to U.S. higher education. In M. S. McPherson, M. O. Schapiro, and G. C. Winston (Eds.), *Paying the piper: Productivity, incentives, and financing in U.S. higher education.* Ann Arbor: University of Michigan Press.

Schilling, K. M., and Schilling, K. L. (1998). *Proclaiming and sustaining excellence: Assessment as a faculty role.* ASHE-ERIC Higher Education Report (vol. 26, no. 3). Washington, DC: Graduate School of Education and Human Development, The George Washington University.

Schmidt, P. (1999, July 2). Government and politics: A state transforms colleges with "performance funding." *Chronicle of Higher Education.* (www.chronicle.com)

Schulz, W. G. (1996). Alliance of industry, academia, labor leads skill standards movement. *Chemical and Engineering News, 74*(35), 39–41.

Serban, A. M. (1998a). Opinions and attitudes of state and campus policymakers. In J. Burke and A. Serban (Eds.), *Performance funding for public higher education: Fad or trend?* (pp. 69–84). New Directions for Institutional Research, no. 97. San Francisco: Jossey-Bass.

Serban, A. M. (1998b). Performance funding criteria, levels, and methods. In J. Burke and A. Serban (Eds.), *Performance funding for public higher education: Fad or trend?* (pp. 61–67). New Directions for Institutional Research, no. 97. San Francisco: Jossey-Bass.

Shepko, R., and Douglas, B. (1998, December). Reframing for crisis. *NACUBO Business Officer.* Washington, DC: National Association of College and University Business Officers. (www.nacubo.org/website/members/bomag/9812/benchmarking.html)

Singleton, R. A., Jr., Straits, B. C., and Miller Straits, M. (1993). *Approaches to social research* (2nd ed.). New York: Oxford University Press.

Snow, R. E. (1974). Representative and quasi-representative designs for research on teaching. *Review of Educational Research, 44,* 265–291.

Spanbauer, S. J. (1992). *A quality system for education.* Milwaukee, WI: American Society for Quality Control Standards.

Steele, J. M., and Lutz, D. A. (1995). *Report of ACT's research on postsecondary assessment needs.* Iowa City, IA: American College Testing.

Steers, R. M. (1975). Problems in measurement of organizational effectiveness. *Administrative Science Quarterly, 20,* 546–558.

Stein, R. B., and Fajen, A. L. (1995). Missouri's funding for results initiative. In G. H. Gaither (Ed.), *Assessing performance in an age of accountability: case studies* (pp. 77–90). New Directions for Higher Education, no. 91. San Francisco: Jossey-Bass.

Stevens, J., and Hamlett, B. D. (1983). State concerns for learning: Quality and state policy. In J. R. Warren (Ed.), *Meeting the new demands for standards* (pp. 29–38). San Francisco: Jossey-Bass.

Tannenbaum, S. I., and Yukl, G. (1992). Training and development in work organizations. *Annual Review of Psychology, 43,* 399–441.

Terenzini, P. T. (1989). Assessment with open eyes: Pitfalls in studying student outcomes. *Journal of Higher Education, 60,* 644–664.

Testa, A. M. (1999, November). *Design and delivery of distance delivered competency based degree programs.* Proceedings from the 1999 Assessment Institute. Indianapolis, IN: Western Governors University.

Texas Higher Education Coordinating Board, Community and Technical Colleges Division. (2000). *State-level institutional effectiveness process for Texas community and technical colleges.* Austin: Texas Higher Education Coordinating Board.

Thorndike, R. L. (Ed.). (1971). *Educational measurement* (2nd ed.). Washington, DC: American Council on Education.

U.S. Air Force Academy, Department of Management. (1997). *Accreditation plan.* Colorado Springs: U.S. Air Force Academy.

U.S. Air Force Academy, Department of Management. (1999a). *Assessment program.* Colorado Springs: U.S. Air Force Academy.

U.S. Air Force Academy, Department of Management (1999b). *Candidacy school profile sheet: American Assembly of Collegiate Schools of Business annual report.* Colorado Springs: U.S. Air Force Academy.

U.S. Department of the Air Force. (1993). *Information for designers of instructional systems.* Air Force Handbook 36–2235. Washington, DC: U.S. Government Printing Office.

U.S. Department of the Air Force. (2000). *Developing, Managing, and Conducting Training.* Air Force Instruction 36–2201. Washington, DC: U.S. Government Printing Office. http://web1.deskbook.osd.mil/htmlfiles/DBY_af-10-Careersalpha.asp

U.S. Department of Labor, Secretary's Commission on Achieving Necessary Skills. (1991). *What work requires of schools: A SCANS report for America 2000.* Washington, DC: U.S. Government Printing Office.

U.S. Department of Transportation. (1997a). *Learning and development framework.* (dothr.dot.gov/L&D_Framework/toc1.html; dothr.ost.dot.gov/L&D_Framework/evaltoc.htm)

U.S. Department of Transportation. (1997b). *United States Department of Transportation strategic plan for fiscal years 1997–2002.* (www.dot.gov/hot/dotplan.html)

Vandenberge, D. G. (1995). An undergraduate quality management and control class for engineers. *ASEE Annual Conference Proceedings, 1,* 1229–1233.

Western Association of Schools and Colleges. (1998). *An invitation to dialogue.* Alameda, CA: Western Association of Schools and Colleges. (www.wascweb.org/senior/invite/ dialogue.htm)

Western Association of Schools and Colleges. (1999). *Invitation to dialogue II: Proposed framework for a new model of accreditation.* Alameda, CA: Western Association of Schools and Colleges.

Western Association of Schools and Colleges. (2001). *Handbook of accreditation.* Alameda, CA: Western Association of Schools and Colleges.

Williams, C., and Wall, A. (1999, Fall). Balanced scorecards at the Veterans Benefits Administration. In *The Business of Government* (pp. 2–5). Arlington, VA: PricewaterhouseCoopers Endowment for the Business of Government.

Winer, B. J. (1971). *Statistical principles in experimental design.* New York: McGraw-Hill.

Wolff, R. (2000, January). *Re-visioning WASC accreditation.* Handout from Council for Higher Accreditation Conference, Washington, DC.

Wolverton, M. (1994). *A new alliance: Continuous quality and classroom effectiveness.* ASHE-ERIC Higher Education Report (vol. 23, no. 6). Washington, DC: Graduate School of Education and Human Development, The George Washington University.

Yuchtman, E., and Seashore, S. E. (1967). A system resource approach to organizational effectiveness. *American Sociological Review, 32,* 891–903.

# Name Index

**A**

Adelman, C., 41
Albright, B. N., 1, 7
Alstete, J. W., 2
Aper, J. P., 35, 36
Astin, A., 35
Ayala, F., 35

**B**

Babbie, E., 75
Banta, T. W., 1, 6, 7, 8, 17, 68, 119
Bassi, L. J., 20, 97
Benjamin, R., 13, 16
Bennett, W. J., 50
Bensimon, E., 141
Borden, V.M.H., 1, 68, 71, 119
Bottrill, K. V., 71
Boyer, C., 1, 35
Bracco, K., 8

**C**

Callan, P., 8
Cambridge, B., 39
Campbell, D. t., 75
Carnevale, D., 47, 152
Cavalluzzo, L. C., 13
Chickering, A., 67
Cole, H. P., 75
Cole, J.J.K., 34
Cook, T. D., 75
Cronbach, L. J., 75
Cuver, S. M., 35
Cymrot, D. J., 13

**D**

Diamond, M., 141
Dickinson, T. L., 75
Dill, D., 27, 107, 108, 109, 110, 111
Douglas, B., 141

**E**

Easton, D., 2
El-Khawas, E., 35
Epstein, P., 6
Ewell, P., 1, 2, 35, 44, 50, 117, 147, 149

**F**

Fajen, A. L., 17
Finney, J., 1, 8, 35
Fiske, D. W., 75
French, N., 108, 112

**G**

Gamson, Z., 67
Gardiner, L. F., 2
Gilmore, J. L., 7
Gleser, G. C., 75
Goldsmith, J., 147
Gonczi, A., 42, 47, 152
Gray, G.R.H., 20

**H**

Hamlett, B. D., 1
Harrod, B., 101, 105
Hebel, S., 17
Hedge, J. W., 75
Hinkle, D. E., 35, 36

# Subject Index

accrediting agencies for, 31–32
accrediting agencies of, 31–32, 38, 46
*U.S. News & World Report* ranking of, 31, 35
Historical benchmarking, 74
HMI (Her Majesty's Inspector), 107
"HR speak," 88

# I

Illinois Board of Higher Education, 30
Input measures, 66
Institutional Review Board, 40
Intermediaries
  certifiers of student competencies as, 147
  corporate professional development/training, 92
  role of, 159n.1
  tension between goals of providers and, 63–64
Intermediary assessment
  Model One approach to, 8, 23–28, 45*t*, 46
  Model Two approach to, 8, 23–24*fig*, 28–36, 45*t*, 46
"Invitation to Dialogue" (WASC), 65
ISD (instructional system development), 18–19
ISO 9000, 25–26, 159n.2
ISO organization, 26, 159n.2

# K

Kentucky Council on Postsecondary Education (CPE)
  compliance issues of, 36
  described, 131–133
  Phase One assessment of, 133
  Phase Two assessment of, 133–136
  stakeholder involvement with, 64
  system heterogeneity of, 57
  *2020 Vision* of, 131, 132, 133, 134, 136
Kentucky State Higher Education Board, 64
*Kids Count* rankings (Kentucky), 72
Kirkpatrick model, 70, 95–96*t*, 104
Kiviat, 16
KSAs (knowledge, skills, and abilities), 153

# L

*Learning from Audit* reports, 110
Level of authority factor, 53–54
Level of resources factor, 54–55
Lucent Learning Performance Center (LPC)
  described, 100
  Phase One assessment of, 101–103
  Phase Two assessment of, 103–105
  resource allocation by, 17–18
Lucent Technologies, 15, 16

# M

Malcolm Baldrige National Quality Award, 6, 29, 32–34, 109
Mann, R. B., 13
Measures
  academic audits quality/productivity, 112–113
  balanced scorekeeping, 141, 143, 145
  choosing, 68–70
  comparison with external peers, 71–72
  comparison with internal peers, 73–74
  comparison with past performance, 74
  comparison with present standards, 73
  developing corporate professional development/training, 93–95, 97
  evaluate performance using, 71–74
  input, 66
  of Kentucky CPE quality/productivity, 135–136
  Kirkpatrick model, 70, 95–96*t*, 104
  LPC quality and productivity, 104–105
  outcome, 67–68
  process, 66–67
  productivity, 94
  selected after setting goals, 77, 79
  of state board quality and productivity, 118–119
  of student competencies certifiers quality/productivity, 151–153
  of Texas Higher Education Coordinating Board quality/productivity, 127–130*t*

Student competencies certifiers
  described, 147–148
  Phase One assessment of, 148
  Phase Two assessment of, 148–153
  Western Governors University as,
    152–153
Sun Microsystems, 21, 92
System heterogeneity, 56–58
System-level assessment. *See* Phase
  One/system-level assessment

## T

Tennessee report card systems, 73, 120*t*
Texas Higher Education Coordinating Board
  Academic Performance Indicator System
    developed by, 69
  centralization of operations by, 55–56
  comparing Lucent Learning
    Performance Center with, 18
  examples of goal measurements
    of, 130*t*
  functions/responsibilities of,
    123–125
  Phase One assessment of, 125–126
  Phase Two assessment of, 126–130
  standardized data/course offerings by,
    19–20
Texas Workforce Education Course
  Manual, 125–126
TQM (total quality management),
  109

*2020 Vision: An Agenda for Kentucky's
  System of Postsecondary Education,* 131,
  132, 133, 134, 136

## U

UCSD (University of California of San
  Diego), 138, 141, 143, 144*t*–145*t*
University Grants Committee, 108
University of Phoenix, 37–39, 69–70, 73–74
University of Southern California School of
  Education, 77, 78*t*
Urban Universities Portfolio Project, 6,
  39–41, 72
U.S. Department of Commerce, 33
U.S. Department of Labor, 42, 43
U.S. Department of Transportation
  (DOT), 12, 14, 40
*U.S. News & World Report,* 29, 31, 35, 46,
  53, 64, 72
USC (University of Southern California),
  138, 139–140*t*, 142*t*

## W

Western Association of Schools and
  Colleges (WASC), 65
Western Governors University (WGU), 42,
  43–44, 152–153
Work Keys, 150–151
Workforce improvement, Phase
  One/system-level assessment to improve,
  20–21

# ASHE-ERIC
# Higher Education Reports

The mission of the Educational Resources Information Center (ERIC) system is to improve American education by increasing and facilitating the use of educational research and information on practice in the activities of learning, teaching, educational decision making, and research, wherever and whenever these activities take place.

Since 1983, the ASHE-ERIC Higher Education Report series has been published in cooperation with the Association for the Study of Higher Education (ASHE). Starting in 2000, the series has been published by Jossey-Bass in conjunction with the ERIC Clearinghouse on Higher Education.

Each monograph is the definitive analysis of a tough higher education problem, based on thorough research of pertinent literature and institutional experiences. Topics are identified by a national survey. Noted practitioners and scholars are then commissioned to write the reports, with experts providing critical reviews of each manuscript before publication.

Six monographs in the series are published each year and are available on individual and subscription bases. To order, use the order form at the back of this issue.

Qualified persons interested in writing a monograph for the series are invited to submit a proposal to the National Advisory Board. As the preeminent literature review and issue analysis series in higher education, the Higher Education Reports are guaranteed wide dissemination and provide national exposure for accepted candidates. Execution of a monograph requires at least a minimal familiarity with the ERIC database, including *Resources in Education* and the current *Index to Journals in Education.* The objective of these reports is to bridge conventional wisdom and practical research.

# Advisory Board

# Consulting Editors

*Ensuring Quality and Productivity in Higher Education*

# Recent Titles

# Back Issue/Subscription Order Form

Copy or detach and send to:
**Jossey-Bass, 989 Market Street, San Francisco, CA 94103-1741**

Call or fax toll free!
**Phone 888-378-2537 6AM-5PM PST; Fax 888-481-2665**

| Individual reports: | Please send me the following reports at $24 each |
|---|---|
| | (Important: please include series initials and issue number, such as AEHE 27:1) |

1. AEHE _____

_____

_____

$ _____ Total for individual reports

$ _____ SHIPPING CHARGES: SURFACE

| | Domestic | Canadian |
|---|---|---|
| First Item | $5.00 | $6.50 |
| Each Add'l Item | $3.00 | $3.00 |

For next-day and second-day delivery rates, call the number listed above.

Subscriptions    Please ❑ start my subscription to *ASHE-ERIC Higher Education Reports* at the following rate (6 issues):
U.S.: $130    Canada: $130    All others: $178

$ _____ Total individual reports and subscriptions (Add appropriate sales tax for your state for individual reports. No sales tax on U.S. subscriptions. Canadian residents, add GST for subscriptions and individual reports.)

Federal Tax ID 135593032                    GST 89102-8052

❑ Payment enclosed (U.S. check or money order only)
❑ VISA, MC, AmEx, Discover Card # _____ Exp. date _____

Signature _____ Day phone _____
❑ Bill me (U.S. institutional orders only. Purchase order required.)
Purchase order # _____

Name _____
Address _____

_____

Phone_____ E-mail _____

For more information about Jossey-Bass, visit our Web site at:
www.josseybass.com                    **PRIORITY CODE = ND1**

**Catherine H. Augustine** is an associate behavioral scientist at RAND, where she conducts research on postsecondary educational assessment and the effectiveness of educational programs. Her current projects include a study of postsecondary student assessment, an investigation of the relationships between achievement and class size in the primary grades, and a review of governance structures in higher education systems.

**Roger Benjamin** is president of Council for Aid to Education, an independent subsidiary of RAND. Before joining RAND, Roger was at the University of Minnesota and the University of Pittsburgh, where he combined careers as a political scientist and an administrator. Currently, he is codirecting a research program on restructuring governance in higher education. He is coauthor of *Higher Education—By Design* and *The Redesign of Governance in Higher Education.*

**Tora K. Bikson,** a senior behavioral scientist at RAND since 1976, is recognized for her research on the introduction of advanced communication and information technologies and their effects in varied contexts of use. She recently completed a project to define organizational needs and identify best practices for creating, managing, and distributing digital documents (including compound, multimedia, and interactive documents) among United Nations organizations based in Europe, North America, and South America.

**Susan M. Gates** is an economist specializing in industrial organization, political economy, and applications of economic management principles to public sector organizations. Recent publications address a variety of issues, including higher education as an industry, academic quality and productivity, and human resource efficiencies stemming from competitive sourcing competitions in the Department of Defense.

**Tessa Kaganoff** conducts education policy research for RAND. She is currently working on a project for the Department of Defense Office of the Chancellor for Education and Professional Development to develop measures to ensure the academic quality of educational providers within his purview.

As part of this project, she is studying exemplary higher education systems and other analogous entities such as accrediting agencies and corporate universities as models for developing standards. She has also been involved in several large-scale program evaluations during her tenure at RAND, including work on the national evaluation of the Learn and Serve America higher education program for the Corporation for National Service.

**Dina G. Levy** is a behavioral scientist working mainly on issues in education, training, and the assessment of human performance. She is currently participating in projects on governance for quality assurance in higher education and on postsecondary student assessment. Other RAND studies she has contributed to include studies on quality and productivity assessment and strategic planning for Department of Defense civilian and professional development, a project aimed at characterizing the future defense workforce, an analysis of the personnel policy implications of Army distance learning, and the design of training for Army logisticians.

**Joy S. Moini** has been a research assistant in RAND's Santa Monica and Washington, D.C., offices while a student. She has been involved in a range of projects focused primarily on education and training issues. Currently, she is involved in a study for the Department of Defense Office of the Chancellor for Education and Professional Development, which is focusing on issues of strategic planning, academic quality and productivity, and governance. She is also working on a project for the Department of Education's Office of Educational Research Improvement looking at the need to establish strategic programs of research in the field of education.

**Ron W. Zimmer** is an associate policy analyst who has published and worked on projects in the field of education, including privatization of education, production of education, financing education, and the interaction of students in a classroom.